12:00
PH
DX-479641

MUDDLING THROUGH: The Art of Properly Unbusinesslike Management

CARTOONS by HENRY MARTIN

ROGER A. GOLDE

MUDDLING THROUGH: The Art of Properly Unbusinesslike Management

amacom A DIVISION OF AMERICAN MANAGEMENT ASSOCIATIONS

Library of Congress Cataloging in Publication Data

Golde, Roger A
  Muddling through.

  1. Management. 2. Organization. I. Title.
HD31.G568   658.4   76-888
ISBN 0-8144-5411-9

© 1976 AMACOM
A division of American Management Associations, New York.
All rights reserved. Printed in the United States of America.

This publication may not be reproduced, stored in a retrieval
system, or transmitted in whole or in part, in any form or
by any means, electronic, mechanical, photocopying, recording,
or otherwise, without the prior written permission of AMACOM,
135 West 50th Street, New York, N.Y. 10020.

First Printing

LET'S TALK ABOUT WHAT GOES WITHOUT SAYING: A Preface

> Sciences . . . give us only that much of
> fact, truth, or well-grounded opinion
> which answers the questions which
> scientists choose to address to their
> subjects. . . . The fault—when fault
> there is—consists of failure to question
> the questions.
> JOSEPH J. SCHWAB, *Private Lives*

In some way each chapter of this book raises certain questions about a part of established management theory. Those who formally write, teach, or speak about management may find the ideas in this book very unbusinesslike—that is, unorthodox or even heretical. Those who practice the craft of management are likely to find the thoughts much less strange, and quite *properly* unbusinesslike.

From one point of view, each of the first six chapters is separate and self-contained. You can feel free to start with whatever chapter piques your curiosity and then roam around as your interest dictates. The chapter topics represent my arbitrary selection of some important and pressing issues—issues which aren't talked about very much but which create serious headaches.

From another point of view, the chapters of this book are all about very much the same things: the fuzzy, chaotic, imprecise, ambiguous, or nonlogical aspects of managerial life. The chapters deal with such unspeakable questions as these: How can you get there when you don't know where you're going? How can you manage when you don't know what you're doing? What can you do when you get stuck?

The first chapter, which describes some techniques for muddling, should put you in a receptive mood for contemplating the less orderly faces of management. The final chapter is a more general treatment of muddling and the fuzzy character of management. Between these two chapters lie a number of more focused forays into what might be called the "twilight zone" of management. Talking about the fuzzy, jumbled aspects of management isn't easy, which of course is one reason why they aren't talked about very much. This book is only an initial exploration of a large and uncharted territory. I do not have all the answers; I don't even have all the questions. If the book seems assertive, it is only my way of provoking you, the reader, into joining the exploration. If the book appears one-sided, it is merely my effort to counterbalance the overwhelming weight of the management literature on the other side.

Throughout the book I have taken the liberty of referring to a manager as "he" or "him" in keeping with the convention of using masculine pronouns to denote a person of either sex. I find it simply too distracting and awkward to refer continually to "he or she" or to use a term such as "management person." At some point, I suppose we may develop a less prejudicial set of terms to replace those we now have. (Even the words "*man*ager" and "*man*agement" smack of the male gender, although in fact they come from the Latin "manus" meaning "hand.") For the present, I can only beg the indulgence of those who feel as I do that women and men should have equal claim to the joys and frustrations of managerial life.

Before plunging into the "fuzz," I want to express my gratitude for the valuable comments and reactions I received along the way from my clear-headed friends: Anthony Athos, Diana Barrett, Robert Guttentag, Constantine Joannidis, Robert Pritchard, and Judy Wortham. I should also like to thank the many managers with whom I have worked over the years. It is their struggles and successes that really provided most of the ideas and inspiration for this book.

Roger A. Golde

CONTENTS

MUDDLING THROUGH: The Art of Properly Unbusinesslike Management

1:
ORGANIZED MUDDLING:
The Art of Thinking in
Straight Circles

BOGGLING

JOE: Hello, I'm Joe King—your host on the "Morning-After Show." At this time I want you all to welcome our first guest, Dr. B. B. Bumble—a formerly successful executive who is now one of the few authorities in the field of boggling. Doctor, why don't you tell us in your own words a little about your "quasi-research," as you call it.

DR. B.: Well, Joe, I guess some people have used other words to characterize our work, but basically we have spent many hundreds of hours in the field seeking out cases of boggling.

JOE: And have you found a lot of it?

DR. B.: Well, that's hard to say because, you know, not too many people are going to tell you right off that they're boggled.

JOE: Sure, I can understand that. By the way, Beebee (if I may call you that), just exactly what is boggling?

DR. B.: Joe, it's sort of hard to describe . . . uh . . . well . . . we haven't really come up with a good definition . . . er . . . I guess you might say we're kind of stuck on that one.

JOE: Well I don't want to put words in your mouth, but could it be that what you mean by boggling is "being stuck"?

DR. B.: Hey, that's not bad! I think we ought to fly with that one. Say, you're not interested in doing a bit of moonlighting as a researcher with us, are you?

JOE: Thanks, anyway, but this job keeps me pretty busy. Tell me, Beebee, aren't there some things you've learned to spot as key indicators of boggling?

DR. B.: Of course—like for instance we look for someone who's running around in circles without getting anywhere. By the way, we have a lot of data on the size and shape of such circles.

JOE: Great, but I don't think we have time right now to go into the shape of circles. What else do you look for?

DR. B.: Well, there's our now-famous "grab count," where we observe and categorize the unsuccessful grabs a manager makes when he hunts for the handle to a problem.

JOE: I think I'm beginning to get a grip on your approach. Are there any other techniques you'd like to tell us about?

DR. B.: Yes, indeed, Joe. For one thing, we spend a lot of time getting boggled ourselves. By doing this, we get a really good idea of what boggling is like from the inside.

JOE: Yeah, I sort of had a hunch about that. Dr. Bumble, thank you so much for coming on the show. I'm not just being complimentary when I say that you have really boggled us all!

Despite Dr. Bumble, boggling is serious business. Boggling is alive and well and living with management in all functions from research to recruiting, from planning to production. Most of the managers with whom I have worked seem to boggle from time to time, and I confess to boggling frequently myself.

Yet boggling certainly is not a common topic of discussion on the job or even in the more esoteric preserves of a management seminar. This is partly because boggling is not a pleasant experience. None of us likes feeling "stuck"; besides, managers aren't *supposed* to get stuck. We may simply not like to admit we are boggled. And even if we want to talk about boggling, our words and language do not lend themselves well to such a task. In fact, talking about boggling may itself be a sort of boggling.

No doubt each of us gets stuck on different problems. What is sticky for me may not turn out to be sticky for you. But the ways in which people boggle do seem to fall into at least two distinct categories. With all due credit to Dr. Bumble, I call the two types of boggling "handle-hunting" and "circle-running." Because the linguistic problems of talking about boggling make it difficult to provide nice, concise definitions, I will describe each form of boggling in several ways from several different perspectives (which, by the way, is not a bad technique for getting unboggled—but more about that later).

Handle-Hunting

Sometimes we can't "get a handle" on a situation because we don't know what we're looking for. The problem is that we don't really know what the problem is. We do feel that something needs fixing; we would like to get some data but we may not know exactly what data are needed; we might not even recognize a good answer to the problem if we stumbled on one. For example, in 1973 and for several years thereafter the task of constructing a federal energy program seemed to boggle a great many people. We all agreed that there was an energy problem, but we did not really know very specifically what that meant, let alone how to deal with it.

Handle-hunting often seems to arise in situations that are super-complex. Complexity is caused in part by the number of bits and pieces that have to be strung together. The sheer magnitude of a major problem can create mind-boggling complexities.

For instance, developing a market strategy for distributing a product or service nationally is much more complex than plotting a distribution strategy for just one local area.

But complexity also involves the *variety* and *interrelatedness* of the bits and pieces of a situation. For example, the market strategy of a conglomerate may be very complex because the firm manufactures many different products sold to a variety of customers through a number of channels. In this case variety is creating complexity. A highly integrated company, however, may also have a very complex market strategy. In this case the interrelated nature of different divisions and products is generating complexity.

Complexity can overwhelm us. The circuits become overloaded and we boggle. There are too many factors to deal with, too much knowledge to assimilate, too many things unknown or uncertain. Above all we have trouble sensing the structure of the situation, and we lack a procedure for tackling the fuzzily perceived problem. Pieces of the problem may lie all around us, but we do not see all of them clearly; we do not know how to fit together the pieces we do see.

Our own deep personal involvement in a situation often contributes to the complexity (and related boggling). When we have a highly personal stake in the resolution of a problem, we must cope with the complex entity of our own being. We must deal with our vast storehouse of so-called facts plus our attitudes and emotions as well. We utilize many different mental processes that go on at many levels (conscious, preconscious, and unconscious). In other words, our own entity represents a highly varied and heavily interrelated set of elements. Thus, problems we care about personally may be far more complex than many apparently complicated problems in which we do not have as great a personal stake.

Handle-hunting is most likely to occur at the beginning of a project, when we are starting to deal with some new kind of situation—a situation sufficiently different that it does not seem to fit into any existing "mental suitcase." For instance, basic research is often one kind of activity in which (by definition) we do not really know what we are looking for. Long-range planning also frequently induces boggling of the handle-hunting variety. The vast panoply of the future lies fuzzily before us, yet the essence of planning is to consider new directions and contemplate potential forces or events in that future.

Circle-Running

In circle-running we get stuck in the same groove. We are in a rut, as they say. Perhaps a problem seems pretty clear and the criteria for judging progress look well defined, but we just cannot find an acceptable answer.

In fact, circle-running can occur precisely because we have overstructured the situation; the boundaries we have set up are too tight and we keep bumping into them at every turn. None of the alternatives seem satisfactory—we look at the same possibilities over and over again, somehow hoping that suddenly one of them will turn out to fit. A cartoon (by Samuel H. Gross) that appeared in *The New Yorker* nicely captures the essence of the situation: A doleful-looking man is seated on the only chair in a barren room. On one wall is a door bearing the instruction "DO NOT ENTER." On the opposite wall is another door with a sign stating "DO NOT EXIT."

To fully reflect the frustration of circle-running, I could add to the doleful man's dilemma by putting up another placard with the directive "DO NOT STAY IN THIS ROOM."

Circle-running makes us feel trapped and hemmed in. We are in the double bind of "damned if we do and damned if we don't." We find ourselves trying to meet contradictory requirements (increasing production and reducing the payroll) or trying to fulfill conflicting values (remaining loyal to the boss when doing so appears to unfairly harm a subordinate who has been doing a good job).

Alternatively, the goals and values may be quite compatible but we may simply see no way to fulfill them. For example, some years ago the Kimberly-Clark Company got stuck on the problem of reducing costs for the distribution of Kleenex. The company had very carefully analyzed the possibility of alternative channels of distribution, the costs of transportation, different kinds of packaging material, and so on. None of these areas suggested any realistic way of cutting distribution costs. (The way Kimberly-Clark broke the boggle and the solution they arrived at are treated later in this chapter.)

Sometimes our options can seem very circumscribed because there are so many factors beyond our control, or because we control too few of the really critical variables. At other times our personal involvement in the problem makes it difficult to realize that we have set artificial boundaries resulting in circle-running.

Circle-running usually sets in after a problem has been worked on for some time, after we are fairly clear about what we are trying to accomplish, have collected a lot of information, and have carefully analyzed a number of obvious alternatives. Breaking out of the "circle" is often referred to as creative or innovative problem-solving—that is, there is a feeling of newness, inventiveness, or imagination evident in the solution that is finally uncovered.

Muddling

Muddling is closely related to boggling, and both are serious business. Yet muddling, like boggling, is rarely discussed. If boggling is taboo, then muddling is at the very least a somewhat tainted management activity. Sex used to be viewed in much the same way—everyone spent a lot of time involved in the activity or worrying about it, but very few were willing to talk openly about it, let alone figure out how to do it better.

Few of us enjoy being boggled for very long; it's just too uncomfortable. Besides, life and the job go on, and we rarely can afford to spend much time sitting paralyzed and stuck. The primary way to stop boggling is to start muddling.

Most managers do muddle, and more frequently than they would like to admit. (Even whole organizations can be said to muddle, although this chapter focuses more on the muddling of an individual manager.) Some managers, however, are better at muddling than others—and for that matter, some jobs seem to require more muddling than others. Typically, the higher up the organization pyramid we look, the more muddling we are likely to find (and this observation should not be taken as an adverse commentary on executive ability at the senior levels). It may even be that the ability to muddle well is somewhat correlated with career advancement.

Yet muddling is difficult to define, and I will defer any rigorous attempt at definition until the last chapter. For now, let us just say it is conscious but nonlogical thinking.

It is also difficult to know or describe precisely how an individual muddles. It is possible, however, to observe a few of the things that managers *do* as they muddle. The rest of this chapter is devoted to such observations, starting first with some of the apparent overall strategies and then singling out some of the more specific tactics that seem to help managers in the muddling process.

MUDDLING STRATEGIES

Strategic Withdrawal
(*Better Known as "Beating a Hasty Retreat"*)

You have no doubt seen those devilish little puzzles that require taking apart two linked pieces of metal shaped like complicated paper clips. One or two of these puzzles is always sitting around in my office where some unwitting visitor can pick them up and start fiddling with them. Usually the visitor boggles quite quickly, turns to me with a sheepish grin, and hands me the puzzle to do, saying, "I give up."

A manager who boggles over one of his tasks may also decide to give up, though rarely in a manner as straightforward or explicit as that of my "puzzled" office visitor. For instance, a manager may simply decide to ignore the boggling situation in the hope that it will go away or somehow take care of itself— and of course sometimes it does.

Instead of simply ignoring the boggle, a manager may try to avoid it by assigning the boggle a relatively low priority or perhaps by explaining that the problem really isn't one. If the boggle is not so easy to avoid, then the manager may resort to putting it off. One way to put off a boggle is to push it off to some indefinite future date because "there just isn't enough time to deal with it at the moment." For example, I often leave a letter unanswered for several months. When I finally do get around to answering it I apologize for the delayed reply, blaming it on my busy schedule. In truth, however, I may have put off answering the letter because I simply couldn't think of what to say or how to say it— in essence, a minor case of boggling. Where more serious affairs are involved, this approach has sometimes been called the art of premeditated crisis—the manager knows the crisis is coming but he doesn't do anything about it until it becomes in fact an unavoidable crisis.

If a manager cannot put off a boggle to the future, then he may be able to put it off on someone else—usually a subordinate, but sometimes another department. Another very common put-off tactic is to call for more research or data collection.

Putting off a boggle can sometimes help. What boggles us now may not boggle us later on; something that boggles me, may not boggle you. If we can stall a boggle for even a little while, there is a fair chance that other important situations will come along and we can lose or bury the boggle among the new problems clamoring for attention. Thus, for example, the furor and boggling over the problems of ecology and the environment in the early seventies became somewhat buried under the subsequent issues of energy, inflation, and recession which came to the fore in the mid-seventies.

These approaches for retreating from a boggle remind me of the new military tank invented by one of the smaller nations. It has three reverse gear speeds—for retreating; and one forward gear speed—in case of attack from the rear. Ignoring, avoiding, or putting off a boggle is fundamentally an attempt to muddle *around* the situation or problem rather than muddle *through* it. The premise is that not taking action minimizes the chances of making a mistake or, more importantly, of being accused of making a mistake.

There is nothing wrong with muddling around, if it works (for both you and the organization). Sometimes the best way to deal with an impasse is to go around it. Sometimes the nature of external pressures and events is such that muddling through is simply not a viable option. But there is also such a thing as irresponsible muddling around—that is, just taking the easy way out. It is often hard to distinguish whether muddling around is responsible or irresponsible because the two look much the same.

Unfortunately, many boggles do not respond well to muddling around. Some boggles may accept being temporarily ignored, but insist on returning later with even greater powers to paralyze and perplex. All too often, muddling around only results in our facing a never-ending series of daily brushfires.

Some boggles refuse to be ignored, even temporarily; they will not leave when asked, and they clamor for immediate attention. Some action is necessary if only to provide temporary relief from the nagging symptoms. It can become more important to move away from the uncomfortable, undesirable situation than to worry about the exact direction in which we are heading; any decision may be better than no decision. We must turn to strategies other than those of withdrawal.

Force-Fitting

In force-fitting we grab an existing handle and stuff the boggle into a suitcase already attached to the handle. We do not choose just any suitcase—we try to pick one that worked for seemingly similar kinds of problems in the past. For example, suppose sales are down and we don't really understand why. We may still go ahead and lower prices (or perhaps raise them) because that "bag" has worked to stop declining sales in the past. We may choose a suitcase simply because it is the favorite of someone important and influential in the organization (in hopes that such a choice will make it more difficult to blame us if the approach does not work).

Often these existing suitcases represent arbitrary rules or procedures. For example, suppose a manager finds it necessary to cut expenses substantially. He may find it a boggling proposition to analyze carefully each area of his operation to determine exactly where the "fat" is. Instead, the manager simply makes a 10 percent cut in all budgeted expenditures across the board.

Of course, the problem with force-fitting is that the boggle does not fit into the suitcase very well. We may have to push the problem all out of shape or else resort to major surgery by lopping off a few limbs of the situation. Force-fitting can be a very productive form of muddling if we sincerely try to mold *both the suitcase and the problem over time* so that the force fit gradually improves. We must realize that the initial fit is not a good one and represents merely a way to get moving. All too often, instead of altering the force fit as we go, we merely devote ourselves to the task of making the initial fit turn out right; we may even adopt the strategy of simply blaming other people and subsequent events for the inadequacy of the fit.

Fragmentation

Fragmentation is a sort of compromise between ignoring a boggle and force-fitting it. Certain parts of the situation are ignored and various pieces of the problem are singled out for attention— pieces which fit nicely into an existing suitcase. For instance, in preparing an annual budget a manager may not be asked to justify every item (so-called "zero-based budgeting") because it would simply be too complex and time-consuming. Instead, the manager is required to justify only items that represent additions to or deletions from the previous year's budget.

Fragmentation as a form of muddling means avoiding any systematic attempt to deal with the whole situation. Many pieces of the problem are never dealt with at all, and there may be little effort to fit together those pieces which *are* dealt with. The fragmentation approach can be a very helpful form of muddling so long as we do not forget that the rest of the situation is still hanging around and not necessarily improving with age.

MUDDLING TACTICS

It has been jokingly observed that "Anybody can plan, but it takes great management to leap from crisis to crisis." In the context of muddling, this statement may be as accurate as it is amusing. There is something inherently contradictory about discussing strategies for muddling, because if we could actually develop and follow a clear, overall strategy we probably wouldn't be truly muddling. In a way, the essence of muddling may be precisely this absence of an explicit, comprehensive strategy for approaching a problem or situation. A muddler may be effective precisely because of his ability to operate without an overall plan or strategy. Thus, the real key to organized muddling probably resides more at the level of tactics than strategy.

Managers who are good at muddling seem to have a varied repertory of techniques on which they can call when they find their natural muddling process has resulted in a boggle. Yet many good muddlers are not able to state explicitly the specific techniques they use. They may not even be aware of them. By isolating and describing some of these tactics, I hope to make them more readily available for use by all managers.

It is difficult to prescribe exactly when and where each of these techniques should be used; probably each manager will use the assortment of techniques differently. So in a sense the rest of this chapter is a kind of grab bag to which you can turn when your usual approaches fail you.

You Never Start from Nowhere

The standard techniques for problem-solving involve such steps as defining the problem, listing objectives, generating alternatives, and somehow selecting among the alternatives. But boggling results precisely because you are unable to define the problem or objectives clearly, or else because none of the alternatives seem satisfactory. So the standard techniques for problem-solving are not much help in getting unboggled; in fact, you may only boggle yourself more by trying to apply them. Yet boggling means being stuck or paralyzed, so starting (or restarting) the muddling process is often difficult.

There is, however, always one sure way to get your muddling started: Temporarily stop trying to solve the problem and *simply state "where you are at."* Of course, the statement of where you are at should be slightly more detailed than merely "I'm boggled." Describing where you are at can and should include statements about the barriers you keep running into, or about what seems to be making the situation so difficult to cope with. You might even state your feelings and emotions about being boggled— indeed, this is often the best place to start. Do you feel frustrated, angry, resentful, helpless, fearful, confused, sad? Such feelings drain off a lot of energy and can create much of the clutter that leads to continued boggling. Not that merely realizing you are, let us say, fearful will necessarily make you any less afraid; but you may then find yourself beginning to pin down just what you fear, or why you are particularly scared now (when you weren't a few weeks ago), and so forth. Stating your feelings to yourself in this way should not be viewed as a form of self-administered psychotherapy, but rather as a "soft-nosed" (as opposed to hard-nosed) way to move off dead center.

Another important part of stating where you are at is to *describe carefully and explicitly what you know* (or think you know) about the problem or situation. If you are handle-hunting,

clarifying what you know can help you construct at least part of a handle. You begin to see that you do know *some* things; you begin to pinpoint which areas are really fuzzy. If you are circle-running, you can apply the same technique, although it will work in quite a different way. As you try to identify what you really know, you are likely to discover that you are relatively sure of very little. You begin to spot assumptions that need to be checked out. You may discover some alternatives that were rejected for inadequate reasons, and you may even think of something that hadn't occurred to you before.

Another productive way to describe where you are at is to identify what you *don't* know about the situation or problem. This is far from an exercise in futility. You will make explicit some things you only vaguely felt you didn't know, and you may find some of the fuzzier aspects of the situation coming into sharper focus.

Stating where you are at often seems too simple to be of much use, or you may feel you already know more or less where you stand. But explicitly stating your feelings and what you know (or don't know) about a problem subtly forces you to look at the situation in a slightly different way. Describing where you are at can help even if you don't see exactly how it's going to help when you start out. (That's one of the basic characteristics of muddling.) In any case, starting with where you are at is something you can always *do;* and doing something can be very important. The key to muddling through is that *one thing leads to another.*

Don't Bottle Up the Boggle (*in Your Head*)

Imagine that somehow a tape recording could be made of the thoughts going on inside the head of a manager who is boggled. If that recording were transcribed, the result might be something like this:

"Well, you know the heart of the problem is still N."

"Yeah, but there's just no way to deal with that."

"Okay, but what I'd really like to do is Y, and that just isn't possible."

"Right, and don't forget about taking A, B, and C into consideration."

"I just don't know what to do; the only answer seems to be Y."

"But you know that won't work!"

"All right, then, I suppose I could always do Z."

"Sure, but that won't handle D and E."

"It's just that damn N factor, and by the way I ought to deal with F and G as well."

"But wouldn't Y take care of F and G? Oh hell, I guess it's just ridiculous to contemplate doing Y."

"Well what about using X? That might take care of A and B."

"Yeah, but X still wouldn't solve the N problem."

Et cetera, et cetera, et cetera.

It has probably taken you less than 20 seconds to read this brief excerpt of a manager's internal dialogue, and I suspect you were well on the way to boggling yourself. You can see how easy it is to become (or stay) boggled if you try to work exclusively within the confines of your own head. One of the causes of boggling in the first place is that the brain has a limited processing capacity. Some research studies have concluded that the brain cannot deal very effectively with more than five to nine pieces of information. (Even the seven digits of a phone number can give us a lot of trouble.) The previous tape excerpt dealt with eleven concepts, as represented by the letters *A, B, X,* and so on.

Even at the beginning of your muddling process it can be very useful to externalize your thinking. One way to do this is to talk out loud—to yourself or even a tape recorder if necessary, although talking to someone else is often more productive. The idea behind this approach is nicely illustrated by the manager whose statements were being sharply questioned by a colleague. The manager retorted, "Look, how do I know what I'm thinking until I hear what I say."

Besides hearing what you say, it can be very useful to *see* what you say—*by jotting your muddling down on paper.* Getting the boggle (or parts of it) down on paper is a way to capture and hold still some of the many thoughts coursing through your head. By jotting down problem *N* and ideal solution *Y*, you have them frozen there in front of you. This will help you avoid bringing them up over and over again every few minutes. You reduce the clutter and free up some of those vital processing slots of the brain—which are, after all, limited in number.

Once you have some of your thoughts down in front of you, it is amazing how you can begin to work and play with them. Moreover, your thoughts somehow always seem just a bit different when you look at them in black and white. Such a shift in perspective seems to be a key ingredient of most successful muddling.

Tactical Ground Rules for Muddling

Verbalizing, with or without using pencil and paper, not only changes your perspective. It also inevitably imposes some sort of structure on your muddling, if only because of the syntax of language or the spatial arrangement of items on a piece of paper. This helps organize the muddling. Yet it is fear of such structuring that often inhibits managers from externalizing their muddling; many managers feel very uncomfortable about submitting their vague thoughts to the automatic structuring of spoken or written language.

A friend once asked me if I would meet with a manager named Stacy and try to help Stacy with his career thinking. Stacy had spent the last few years working hard to develop a small business which at last appeared ready to bear fruit. Unfortunately, Stacy's partner in the venture had contrived a way to throw Stacy out of the business, and had done so rather unceremoniously. Stacy was now unemployed.

As I listened to Stacy talk about his career situation, it was clear he did not lack ideas or possibilities or ability. Stacy had a great number of thoughts swirling around in his head, although his thinking was naturally tinged with bitterness about the lost opportunity of his previous venture. Every new possibility seemed to have some fatal flaw such as requiring too much capital or demanding experience or credentials Stacy lacked. In short, Stacy was boggled.

It was obvious that prior to our meeting Stacy had done a good deal of thinking and had talked about his problem with several other people. I asked Stacy if he had any written notes on his previous thinking or conversations. He said he did not. As I launched into a little speech on the virtues of pencil and paper, Stacy quickly interrupted. He said he did not need to be convinced; he often made lists of columns of things to help organize his thinking as he worked on a business problem.

I proceeded to ask Stacy why he had not resorted to his pencil-and-paper habit in dealing with this most complex and crucial career problem. After some reflection, Stacy replied rather sheepishly that he guessed the reason was because *he simply did not know what to make a list of, or what to title his columns.*

This episode dramatically crystalized for me one of the basic barriers to externalizing muddling: feeling you have to follow a specific set of ground rules which are simply not appropriate for muddling. For example:

1. Know what you are trying to say.
2. Establish clear connections between various pieces, especially in terms of cause and effect.
3. Be relatively certain about what you know.
4. Try to minimize chances of making an error.
5. Be reasonably precise and specific.
6. Above all, be consistent.

If you could follow such ground rules, you probably wouldn't need to muddle; in fact, you probably wouldn't have been boggled in the first place. The very purpose of muddling is to find out more about what you know. If you could clearly see all the connections among the pieces of the puzzle, you would already be well on your way toward knowing what to do about the situation.

How can you be sure of what you'll find out from muddling? You can't. You'll inevitably follow some false trails, and you'll often end up in blind alleys. Your written or spoken muddling is likely to appear very imprecise. The odds are that you will be highly inconsistent as you try to juggle all the complexities of the boggling situation.

In a way, muddling is a form of doodling. Many of us find

no difficulty in artistic doodling but are much more inhibited when it comes to doodling with words and ideas. Stacy felt a bit silly writing things down on paper when he knew many of them would not be correct or even helpful. He felt awkward about jotting things down in random order and simply waiting for some order to emerge from his jottings. He somehow felt it was not possible to list things in columns when he did not know in advance what the caption at the top of each column was supposed to be. In short, Stacy was assuming that his use of pencil and paper must conform to a set of ground rules that is simply not designed to assist muddling.

The point is that stating where you are at, externalizing the boggle, and the various techniques which follow can all help organize your muddling. But you'll never get anywhere if you force the techniques to comply with a set of ground rules inappropriate for muddling.

Once-Over-Lightly, Please

Long years of schooling or training in the more orderly forms of problem-solving create a bias toward wading carefully through a whole ball of wax rather than quickly racing once around the track to get the lay of the land (if you'll pardon the mixed metaphors—a technique to be described shortly). Especially in handle-hunting, the once-over-lightly routine can be very useful:

A major management consulting firm received a contract to recommend improvements in the organization of a very large government agency. The initial phase of the study required developing a comprehensive "photograph" of the agency's current mode of operation and its implications for the future. Then various organizational alternatives were to be analyzed.

The agency to be studied provided services in hundreds of locations throughout the United States, employed several hundred thousands of people, and expended billions of dollars annually. The entire consulting project was to be completed within four months and was to involve a team of some 50 consultants. Even to the experienced team of consultants, the project appeared monumental. After several weeks of handle-hunting, most of the consulting team was suffering from a severe case of the boggles.

The project finally got off dead center when the leader decided to make a somewhat incomplete "photograph" in a quick and rather arbitrary fashion. The tactic was to track seven different cycles in the functioning of the government agency, such as a financial cycle from budgeting the request for funds through the receipt and allocation of those funds; a personnel career cycle from recruitment and hiring through promotion or termination; a research and development cycle; and so on.

The team knew that the seven cycles would not represent a complete photograph and might not even be the best way to organize the *final* photograph. The seven cycles, however, did represent a way to get around the track once, quickly.

As it turned out, tracing the cycles led to interviewing many key people at various levels in various management areas and generated some important statistical data as well as some qualitative data about objectives, decision-making methods, and so on. The boggle was broken, and the next steps in the study became much clearer.

One reason you may shy away from the once-over-lightly approach is your fear that it will produce half-baked or incomplete ideas (which in fact it probably will). You may worry about somehow getting committed to these early, inadequate concepts. You may fear that the first go-around will irrevocably shape your subsequent thinking on the situation. As you run around the track for the first time, it may feel strange to ignore some sticky point (for the moment) and move on to complete the circuit. Such reactions and fears are not at all groundless— they're just inappropriate (i.e., those old logical ground rules rearing their ugly heads again in the wrong place). There certainly are risks in the once-over-lightly approach, but unfortunately muddling (as well as other forms of thinking) involves taking a certain amount of risk.

To mix a few more metaphors, you may feel you will lose your shirt by forcing yourself once around the track quickly, but instead you will probably end up with some sort of coatrack on which to begin hanging things. You may even get a handle on what's wrong with the shape of the coatrack.

Incidentally, after you've gotten around the track once, it

can be useful to pull together your ramblings on one or two pages. Managers often use this kind of summarizing technique on a very detailed, thorough analysis, but fail to realize that the same technique can help in muddling. Coping with lengthy notes of the muddling variety (even though captured on paper) can put a great strain on the limited processing capacity of the brain. Too many pages of imprecise, groping notes can make it literally impossible to *see* important relationships and possible handles. The excess verbiage is best kept "out of sight, out of mind."

Shifting Perspective

I am on one side of a four-lane highway with cars whizzing by in both directions. I wish to visit my friend who lives in a house on the other side of the highway directly across from where I am standing. I am afraid to cross the highway because the cars are coming much too fast to see me or stop for me.

I shift my focus from the house and concentrate on the highway and suddenly notice an "island" in the middle. Perhaps I could walk across in two stages, which would make the crossing a little less hazardous.

I turn my attention to the cars whizzing by and notice that every once in a while there seem to be fewer cars. So maybe I could get across during a moment of sparse traffic.

I look to my left down the highway and notice something that looks like a traffic light, way off in the distance. I suppose I could walk to the light and cross the highway there.

Now I glance across the highway again to my friend's house and notice that his car is not in his driveway and some newspapers are stacked up against his front door. He probably isn't even at home and I may not really need to get across the highway at all.

In this little vignette I kept shifting my viewpoint and thus uncovering new aspects of the situation. Shifting my perspective led me to new approaches and helped me make new connections among various pieces of the situation. Of course you could argue that I didn't really find anything new—that is, all the pieces of the situation were already there; I just didn't see them. But isn't that basically the nature of any situation?

A problem-solving procedure is often regarded simply as a way to think about a given, already-perceived situation. In fact, the real usefulness of a problem-solving technique is its ability to *change* the way you perceive a situation—which leads to greater insight and to new ideas for coping with the situation. Your perceptions of a problem inevitably limit your thinking about it. It is hard to ignore the aspects of a situation that you feel, see, or know; and it is well nigh impossible to deal with those parts of a situation which you do not feel, see, or know.

If you can't get unboggled, it may be because your existing perspective blocks you from seeing any appropriate action and because you have run out of obvious ways to change your perspective. Indeed, all the techniques for muddling through are effective in part because they help create or induce some shift in perspective.

Good muddlers utilize a great number of techniques for shifting their perspective, but almost all the techniques can be classified into these three categories:

1. Changing the medium of expression
2. Changing the way a given medium of expression is used
3. Imagining a change in the situation itself

Making one or more of these types of changes will inevitably alter your perspective. Of course the shift in viewpoint that occurs will not necessarily be helpful or lead you to exactly what you need, but then there never are any guarantees when you are muddling.

The remainder of this section gives some specific examples of how you can make each of the three types of change.

THE MEDIUM IS THE MASSAGE (I.E., CHANGING THE MEDIUM)
This technique overlaps somewhat with the tactic of "externalizing the boggle." One way to change the medium in which you muddle is to talk out loud to yourself or someone else instead of silently ruminating inside your head. Pencil and paper provide yet another medium of expression. Incidentally, some managers who type find this to be a rather different medium from hand-

writing; that is, they find themselves thinking quite differently when typing rather than writing in longhand.

Another important medium for muddling is pictures and images, and you don't have to be a Rembrandt to make use of this medium for muddling purposes. Symbols and diagrams (including, of course, numbers but also boxes, circles, arrows, charts, and graphs) form yet another set of media which you can use to induce new perspectives.

As a simple example, take the fluctuations of your favorite stock on the New York exchange, and think about the different insights you might gain from viewing the data in each of the following different media:

—A stock analyst's verbal description of the historical price movement of the stock.

—A numerical listing of the stock's daily closing prices.

—A line chart or graph of the stock's closing prices.

—A comic strip drawing of someone blowing up a balloon (perhaps with hot air?) to represent increases in the stock price, and letting air out of the balloon to represent declines in the price. (All the while in the background of the picture is an evil-looking man prowling around with a long hatpin.)

Translating your muddling from one medium to another encourages you to see the situation differently because each medium of expression has its own built-in structure; each medium has its own somewhat unique set of capabilities and limitations; and each medium gives its own special rubdown to the data. Even if you won't go as far as Marshall McLuhan did in claiming that "The medium is the message," you will find it difficult to argue with McLuhan's own perversion of his dictum, "The medium is the massage."

MASSAGING THE MEDIUM (I.E., CHANGING THE USE OF A GIVEN MEDIUM)

There are obviously a great many ways to use (or massage) each medium to tease out new insights. Just look at how varied the prose of different authors can be. Language can be humorous, cynical, terse, emotional, mystical; the list goes on and on. I will restrict myself to describing just two particularly productive ways of massaging the medium of language (although the techniques can be usefully applied to many other media).

The first technique involves changing the level of abstraction at which you talk or think about the problem situation; that is, *you try describing things either in a more abstract or a more specific way.* Here is an example of moving to more general terms:

A production manager could not figure out what to do with all the spiral coils of metal waste being turned out in his machine shop. By trying to think of the pieces of scrap in more general terms he noted that they were bright, lightweight, inexpensive, fireproof, and available in large quantities.

Now in one sense such abstractions seem to move the production manager away from his specific problem; to some degree, making an abstraction always means omitting some specific details. But, like viewing a landscape from a hilltop, an abstraction allows you to shift your horizon and see new relationships among parts of the countryside. The production manager's abstractions finally did give him a new idea: He convinced his company to sell the spiral coils of waste as Christmas tree icicle ornaments.

In the following example, moving to a more specific level helps organize the muddling:

A personnel director had scheduled two meetings with key line managers who wanted to discuss problems of motivating subordinates. The personnel director decided to focus the discussion of the first meeting around the concept of certain basic needs that everyone has for security, esteem, self-fulfillment, and so forth. While the managers did seem to grasp the idea of these various needs, somehow the meeting did not get anywhere. The managers were not clear about how to apply these need concepts and jokingly observed that they would all need to get degrees in psychology before they could diagnose their subordinates' needs.

In thinking about what to do at the second session, the personnel director felt he ought to tackle the problem of motivation a bit differently, but found it hard to come up with another meaningful approach. He consciously tried to force himself to be more specific. He noted that subordinates after all don't go around talking about security and esteem. What *do* they talk and gripe about?

After some muddling the personnel manager came up with a list of such things as "wanting more time with the boss" and "expecting a word of thanks when extra effort is given." These seemed to be the kind of specifics that subordinates (and bosses) really thought about. Using these specifics as the basis for the second meeting really perked things up. This level of specificity hit the managers where they lived.

If you don't know whether to get more abstract or more specific, just try to move in one direction or the other and you will usually get a rather quick gut reaction as to whether you are moving in the right direction. Sometimes it is the forest you can't see for the trees, and at other times it is the trees you can't see for the forest.

The other technique of massage I want to describe involves *using a medium very loosely instead of very literally.* For instance, similes, metaphors, and analogies are used all the time in language. These figures of speech have the power to conjure up images and emotions which can suggest new ways to look at a situation. For instance, just see how different the images are that flit through your head in response to each of these terms: *prospecting; tilling virgin soil; bringing religion to the heathen.* Yet any one of these phrases could be used as a metaphor to help describe the activity of selling to new customers.

Managers, most of the time, strive to use very literal, accurate figures of speech. Yet the tighter you make your analogy, the closer it will keep you to the situation as you already know it. Thus, using a "half-apt" analogy is much more likely to induce a shift in perspective. So try forcing yourself to develop comparisons which seem unusual, fanciful, or even poetic. (Poets are always using "far out" metaphors to provoke new insights; they compare things which we would not usually think of comparing.) Your strange comparisons need not capture the whole essence of the problem. Such complete analogies are hard to find, and if they are really complete they may not create much of a shift in viewpoint.

Earlier in this chapter, I mentioned Kimberly-Clark's problem of cutting the distribution costs of Kleenex. I do not know the exact discussion which led to uncovering the ultimate solution. I do know that the Kimberly-Clark group used the technique of metaphorical exploration. Here is a hypothetical example of how the technique might have worked:

One manager commented that efficient transportation reminded him of a vacuum. Such a comment puzzled the other managers (and puzzlement is a reliable sign that the metaphor may help to shift perspective). When pushed to describe what he meant, the manager said he wasn't really sure, but he had read that things move very swiftly in a vacuum because there is no friction or air resistance.

Because the group was tolerant of loose comparisons, they began to play around with the "vacuum" figure of speech. A marketing manager remarked that he couldn't see how to transport Kleenex through a vacuum, but they were certainly shipping around a lot of air. This led someone to suggest vacuum-packing Kleenex, although literally this wasn't a very practical idea. Ultimately the group shaped these notions into the possibility of pressing most of the air out of Kleenex. Such a procedure would save some paperboard costs of packaging as well as reducing the shipping costs and warehousing space because of the smaller bulk.

Today, most Kleenex is in fact packaged in these so-called "space saver" boxes.[1]

IMAGINING A CHANGE IN THE SITUATION ITSELF

The strategies of force-fitting and fragmentation involved actually distorting or changing the situation to fit it into an existing suitcase. Another approach is just to mentally toy with various changes. As with figures of speech, the more dramatic or severe a change you imagine, the more likely you are to shift your perspective on the situation. The technique in some ways

[1] A more detailed description of ways to use loose analogies plus a brief reference to the Kleenex case can be found in George M. Prince, *The Practice of Creativity* (New York: Harper & Row, 1970).

is a bit like looking at yourself in those curved mirrors they have in most amusement-park fun houses; these mirrors often make you highly aware of certain features you might not have noticed much before.

Imagine your problem was a hundred times more serious (or less serious); blow up a small part of the problem until it is very large (just think how different a strand of hair or a piece of newsprint looks through a high-power magnifying lens). What would the situation look like upside down, or inside out, or backwards? [2] In other words, ask a silly question and you may get some novel answers.

The classic application of this technique occurred some years ago in the canned salmon industry. One firm was trying to sell white salmon meat, without much success because all the other canned salmon on the market was pink. The advertising agency for the company decided to try looking at the white color as an asset instead of a liability (i.e., what would the problem look like upside down or backwards?). Finally the company launched a very successful sales and advertising campaign built around this slogan:

OUR SALMON DOESN'T TURN PINK IN THE CAN

Organized Muddling

To sum up, muddling from time to time is unavoidable and sometimes even desirable. Yet the types of muddling that come most naturally to us don't always work as well as we would wish. "Muddling around" falls into this category: It may sometimes provide a good way out, but more often than not it only increases our problems. Knowing how to "muddle through" (as opposed to muddling around) can be a very important part of management, and approaches for muddling through are indeed worthy of explicit attention.

If effective muddling is to some degree an art, it is nonetheless an art that can be consciously cultivated. Yet skill in muddling is unlikely to flourish if muddling remains a tainted activity,

[2] The classic checklist for making such imaginary distortions can be found in Alex Osborn, *Applied Imagination* (New York: Scribner's, 1953).

hidden underground, and rarely discussed openly. If nothing else, I hope this chapter demonstrates the possibility of talking usefully about muddling; I hope the chapter has also established the existence of specific ways to coax and shape the muddling we do.

It is these implications that I wished to suggest by the title phrase for this chapter: Organized Muddling.

2:
IN SUBORDINATION

THE VIEW FROM BELOW

What do you gripe about the most? Probably not your subordinates, but your boss. If you work in any kind of organization, the odds are you are a subordinate and will be one the rest of your working life. Your superior seems to control much of your destiny; he provides only a few of your satisfactions and much of your grief.

Management, you are told, is the technique of accomplishing results through other people. Those other people, however, turn out to be primarily the ones you supervise, at least if you go by the content of the management training courses in your organization or at the nearby business school. Yet the reality is that you must accomplish most of your personal goals, and even those of the organization, through your *superiors*—or perhaps in spite of them.

If the art of being a subordinate is important or difficult, you certainly wouldn't know it by leafing through the management magazines and literature at the local library. Yes, the books talk a lot about subordinates, but the point of view always seems to be that of helping you become a better boss. Admittedly, every now and then a book appears on the art of corporate climbing and conniving, or "How to Succeed in Business by Really Trying." The problem is that once you get promoted you still end up as a subordinate—to some new boss.

This chapter is not about making your way up the organizational ladder, although it might help. Nor is this chapter about how to be a better boss, although it might do exactly that. This chapter does attempt to offer some ideas about how to be a better (and possibly happier) subordinate—in particular, how to better manage and understand your boss.

As subordinates, of course, we have all had bosses and have gotten some inkling of how they really operate. But we still fall prey to what I call "bossology": the endless stream of commentary about strategic planning, effective delegation, careful control, analytical decision-making, appraisal and development of subordinates, and so on. Bossology is a quite compelling and highly seductive part of the popular mythology of management.

As bosses we like to think we stick close to the tenets of bossology; even when we do not, we are skilled at explaining our behavior so as to exemplify the best of bossology. As subordinates we expect the boss to follow the standards set forth in bossology. We prefer to view any deviations from these standards as either temporary lapses or signs of true incompetence. At the very minimum we expect the boss to rate as high as we do on the bossology scale—or else why is he the boss?

HE AIN'T NECESSARILY SO

Reason and logic are central tenets of bossology. Where once these terms implied consideration of only impersonal factors such as products, costs, and profits, they now include consideration of many human factors as well. Ask any manager how he came to make some important decision. You will get a long recital of how he uncovered the problem, collected certain facts, carefully laid out the alternatives, analyzed the pros and cons (including the human factors), and finally reached his decision. In short, you get the textbook model of rational decision-making. Intuition or hunches, biases or prejudices, emotional reactions, and personal needs apparently were exiled to some nether regions from whence they exercised but feeble influence. It is near treason to suggest that ignorance, ambiguity, or inconsistency was part and parcel of the decision-making process. A boss who is not rational, objective, and fair is just not a good boss.

But look, your boss works in the same organization you do—an organization full of people working at cross purposes to fulfill individually differing needs; an organization dealing with issues sometimes so new or complex that they cannot be fully analyzed or understood; an organization dealing with a future that is usually so unexpected no one can really prepare for it. If logic and reason were the only things involved, your boss's job could be performed by a computer and you would be reporting to it, not him. If your boss tried to behave like a computer, he would be quickly reduced to inaction and find himself in a corner stammering "It doesn't compute; it doesn't compute."

On the one hand, *if you try to understand your boss in purely logical terms, you are doomed to failure or frustration.* On the other hand, *you must be careful not to forcibly destroy the fiction that your boss is acting logically.* If you confront your boss with an obvious inconsistency or lack of objectivity, he will feel very uncomfortable and wriggle like crazy to explain away (logically) the apparent discrepancy.

In some fields, no attempt at all is made to explain discrepancies. Consider an example from the world of politics, where the compulsion for rationality is somewhat less pervasive:

A senior congressman was stating his opinion about the reorganization of an important government agency. At one point the congressman's visitor tactfully observed that what the distinguished legislator was now saying seemed to contradict a point he had made a few minutes earlier. The visitor's comment didn't phase the congressman one whit. Without batting an eyelash he swiftly replied, "Well, that's democracy!"

In most nonpolitical situations, it would be unacceptable to make such a response; it would be considered quite arbitrary or highly irresponsible. A "logical" answer must be given—and bosses (like the rest of us) don't like being put on the spot. They feel uncomfortable and tend to resent the people who make them feel that way. You are wise to leave your boss a reasonable way to save face, by coming up with a fact he was not aware of, an alternative he had not considered, or a new way to interpret the figures.

Knowledge—What the Boss Doesn't Know Can Hurt You

Another tenet of bossology is the idea that the boss acts out of knowledge. As a subordinate, you probably assume the boss knows what he wants. The next chapter, on discretion, goes to some length to poke serious holes in this assumption. In brief, the boss often cannot know what he wants and will look to you, the subordinate, to find out for him. Moreover, even if your boss knows what he wants, he can rarely know it completely or specifically enough to provide you with an unambiguous description.

In fact, as you fill in the details and specifics, you affect and even substantially change what your boss wants.

Next, you may assume that the boss knows *you*. You may feel he carps a bit too much about your failings, but basically you believe he has a good idea of your capabilities and potentialities.

If you think about it, though, how *can* you expect your boss to know about your unused skills and abilities? If they are truly unused, they are likely to be unseen as well. And how much can your boss really know about your personal dreams and aspirations; your secret vices; your domestic problems that affect you on the job? Okay, some of these things may not be the proper business of your boss. If your boss is not aware of them, however, it is hardly fair to expect him to take them into account.

Well, if your boss doesn't really know you, at least he ought to know what you are *doing,* how much of a workload you are carrying. After all, he gave you the assignments in the first place. Ah yes, but giving you the assignment doesn't mean knowing what is involved in carrying it out. How much do you really know about the workload of your subordinates—say, your secretary, to make it simple? How much of your secretary's day is occupied with typing, answering the phone, filing, and so forth? How long does it take your secretary to type a page of material, to transcribe a page of dictation? (Too long is not a precise enough answer.) Most managers have only a rough idea of the answers to these questions, and their answers differ greatly from those of their secretaries.

The point is that *your boss probably knows less than you think about you and your work* (which often makes his behavior seem less reasonable than it actually is). The best person to fill him in is you.

Sitting in Judgment

Your boss may not know what he really wants, he may not know you well, and he may not know exactly what you are doing. But after all, what your boss really cares about is results, and he can certainly judge those for himself. Look at all the reports and figures he gets telling him what is happening (admittedly, sometimes a bit late).

Unfortunately, those figures are usually influenced by many factors besides your direct efforts. Moreover, as ·a manager you are supposed to be worrying to some degree about the future, and what you do now to improve the future may not create any tangible results until much later on. Much of what you do as a manager-subordinate does not directly affect any numbers. So how is your boss to know about all those little conflicts you resolved, the new ideas you generated to solve unexpected problems, or all the problems you prevented by thinking ahead?

Of course, an astute boss relies on more than the formal reports he gets. He keeps his ear to the ground and picks up a good deal of news about your activities in other ways—in the elevator, over coffee, or at a meeting (where you are not present). The problem is that these informal reports provide only bits and pieces; they are often second- or third-hand and reflect all the biases and distortions of the grapevine that produced them.

The implications of all this are evident in a comment made by the Massachusetts area vice president of the New England Telephone Company:

> An informal trial in our company suggested that appraisals by the subordinate of the boss are most accurate, appraisals by the boss of the subordinate are less accurate . . . as measured against quantifiable results.[1]

I recall with some fondness an English professor who once gave me an A in a course when I had written only B papers and exams. The professor explained to me that he graded on the basis of his "emotional response." I don't know the extent of this approach in academia, but I suspect it is quite widespread in the field of management.

So the reality is that you probably know more about your triumphs and failures than your boss does. If you care about what your boss thinks of your work, *much of the responsibility*

---

[1] Bruce Harriman, "Up and Down the Communications Ladder," *Harvard Business Review* (September–October 1974).

for getting him the proper data to make a judgment falls to you.
You may have to check to make sure that the hard data do
indeed reflect some of your efforts; if appropriate data do not
exist, you may have to develop some and try to get them into
the system. Similar effort may be required on the less quantifiable
or intangible results of your work. You can fill in your boss
directly, but only to a limited extent, because you are clearly
suspect as a source of favorable comment about your own work.
Your boss is all too well aware of the old saying that "No employee ever expended much effort to prove himself wrong." So
you may have to take some explicit steps to ensure that your boss
hears good news indirectly from others. When something really
has gone wrong, it is not a bad idea to present some of the unhappy news yourself before your boss picks it up from a less
charitable source.

Your boss may be the one who tallies the score and declares
the winners, but you have considerable power to determine at
least some of the bases on which you will be measured and
judged. You ought to exert some of this power, because just
doing what you feel is a good job may not be enough. Your boss
may have a totally different idea of what constitutes "a good job,"
and his natural tendency will be to follow the dictum first attributed to an ancient Greek in the year 20 B.C.: "All men judge
the acts of others by what they would have done themselves."

REWARDS—EASIER TO RECEIVE THAN GIVE

The difficulty the boss has in judging his subordinates affects
the way in which he is likely to hand out rewards. It is risky for
the boss to hand out rewards for results he isn't sure about. Don't
forget the boss's desire to appear fair and objective in front of
the whole pack of subordinates who watch his every move, waiting to squawk at the slightest hint of favoritism (i.e., rewarding
something intangible or not clearly evident). Each subordinate
has his own notion of what is fair. Each subordinate wants to be
"first among equals"—that is, treated equally but just a little bit
more equally than the other subordinates. No wonder bosses
prefer to go by the numbers and base rewards on budgets and

quotas, or else seek the safety of the annual "merit" increases, which are usually more annual than merit-based.

Even when a subordinate has done something clearly and tangibly worthy of reward, the boss may still be reticent to offer proper recognition. In this kind of situation, bosses worry about the future expectations that the subordinate might develop after getting such a reward. One manager in an Eastern electronics firm put it this way:

> If I give one of my subordinates some recognition by taking him to an important meeting, or mentioning his name in a lot of memos, the next thing I know the guy is in my office wanting to know why he didn't get the big raise or promotion he expected.

Help!

As a subordinate you may not see yourself as a "servant," but you may well feel that to some degree you serve your boss. In return you are likely to expect your boss to help you, at least with task-related problems; it seems only fair, since such problems after all arise out of your efforts to serve your boss. The tenets of bossology lead you to expect your boss to warn you about such things as potential problems, sore spots, or traps in an assignment.

Now let us assume that your boss is actually inclined to provide such help. The bind is that your boss is quite unlikely to know what to warn you about. An assignment is often too general at the start to permit easy prediction of potential problems; it is only after you have delved into the specifics of the task that the problems become apparent.

Moreover, your boss probably focuses on the results he wants rather than the problems in getting those results. Emotionally, the boss has considerable motivation to avoid detecting problems which pose significant barriers to the achievement of his goals, and this bias is likely to persist throughout the assignment, not only at the start.

DBMP-BMA

I am told that these mysterious initials once adorned a sign prominently placed on the desk of David Jacquith when he was president of Vega Industries. When a new subordinate came into Jacquith's office to discuss a problem, the subordinate would of course notice the sign and innocently inquire as to its meaning. Jacquith would then explain that the letters stood for the phrase, "Don't Bring Me Problems—Bring Me Answers."

Bosses look to subordinates to take a load off their shoulders. Bringing a problem to your boss increases his load, so his outlook on your job-related problems may not be very charitable to begin with. A job-related problem usually poses some sort of barrier to a goal desired by your boss; the problem may even imply that the goal is not attainable. The problem requires your boss to spend time—time to get to the heart of the matter and time to figure out what the devil to do about it.

As a subordinate you may feel that uncovering key problems is a vital part of your job, and it probably is. But you must realize that *bringing a problem to your boss is not giving him something; it is more like taking away something that he wants* (as well as taking up his time).

Even giving the boss information to digest takes something away from him (i.e., time). And don't forget that the processing capacity of anyone's brain is relatively limited; it can only handle a few things at a time without boggling. Your boss can digest only a limited amount of information on any one problem, and he can cope with only a limited number of problems at any one time. Each piece of information and each problem you bring your boss use up some of that limited capacity. In addition, bosses (like many of us) do not necessarily enjoy hard thinking in the first place. So the more serious or insoluble the problem you give your boss, the more you may be taking away from him.

What is even worse, however, is that if the problem is serious, the boss may have to take some action himself. He may have to risk his own neck or at least expend some of his carefully hoarded "political capital"—all of which, he may feel, might have been avoided if you had only handled the thing (properly) yourself without involving him. To top it all off, your boss may not really know how to handle the problem. So he feels both impotent (which he doesn't like in the least) and angry (quite possibly at you) for having to live with the negative consequences of the problem you brought to his attention.

So spare the boss as much thinking as you can. If you must "take away" something by raising a problem, at least try to give back something in return in the form of a few alternatives that might ameliorate the problem. Over two thousand years ago Sophocles observed that "Nobody likes the bearer of bad tidings."

TRAINING AND DEVELOPMENT

The more recent versions of bossology imply that training and development is another type of help you might expect from your boss. In reality, your boss is likely to view training and developing you as another kind of problem which you bring to him, and generally a problem with which he would prefer not to deal.

Helping someone learn new managerial skills is itself a special skill—a skill not highly emphasized in most courses on bossology. So the boss's lack of formal background in the areas of teaching and learning only adds to his reticence to train and develop you. Moreover, in most organizations, training and development is not the kind of activity that is easily reported or formally evaluated. In light of all this, the boss probably views training and development as a necessary evil, a kind of negative obligation that only drains his energies from other important things he must accomplish—accomplishments on which he will be formally judged.

Publicly the boss may pronounce training and development to be at least as desirable as motherhood and democracy, while privately his attitude may more closely resemble these off-the-record comments from the general manager of an oil-company division:

> I guess it's my feeling that if one of my men is really competent, he doesn't need much training; and if he isn't that competent, then there's probably not much that training can do anyway.

In other words, *it's mostly up to you to help your boss help you.* If you want to develop and grow, you will probably have to shoulder most of the burden for determining specifically what you need and some of the possible ways in which you might acquire the new skills and experience you desire. If you have done some of this hard thinking and then discuss the issues with your boss, you greatly increase the odds that he will be able or willing to help.

The Limits of Boss Power

As a subordinate you may frequently be frustrated by the apparent power and control of your superiors. Being somewhat under the control of others is part of the price paid for belonging to any organization. What you may forget is that your boss must pay similar dues. Even the most powerful top executives rarely control everything they would like to:

The Appropriations Committee of the U.S. House of Representatives is generally considered to be one of the most powerful groups in the Congress because of its role in the fiscal budgeting process. Some years ago I was present at an informal, off-the-record session with the chairman of this committee. I was amazed to hear him spend most of the meeting bemoaning his lack of power and control. The chairman seemed genuinely frustrated by his inability to implement the many reforms he felt were desperately needed in the budgeting process.

Somehow power seems to be a scarce commodity in most organizations. The theorists may debate how to arrange things so that everyone can have most of the power he would like, but all it takes to upset any of their schemes is one manager in the chain of command who acts as if there were not enough power to go around. The attitude quickly spreads through the ranks and effectively guarantees that there will not be enough power for everyone.

So bear in mind that your boss does not control everything he would like to control; your boss is struggling with *his* boss, who may not always be reasonable, knowledgeable, and helping. By the way, when you really think about it, one of the things your boss probably does not fully control is your promotions. Also, your boss cannot give you things he does not have, nor can he give you things he has but does not know how to give. Certain kinds of knowledge and help often fall into these categories.

Now, the boss's lack of control may merely provide him with an excuse to shirk responsibility for problems (both his and yours). In any case, his lack of control is probably a genuine source of annoyance. He can hardly take his irritation out on his superiors; often, the easiest or only place for him to vent his frustrations is in the downward direction, on you. So as a subordinate you must realize that often, as Laura Huxley has written, "You are *not* the target. You just happen *to be* there. . . . Sometimes it is true; people are trying to hurt us. But most of the time they are merely exploding, and we happen to be nearby —a convenient substitute for their *real* target." [2]

The moral to all this is: Be careful what you ask of your boss; don't ask him for something he doesn't have the power to give or something he doesn't control. If you do, you won't really advance your cause and you risk upsetting the boss by indirectly reminding him of his lack of power or some other lack he isn't supposed to have.

THE POWER DIFFERENTIAL

Your boss may not have all the power he would like, but he certainly has power—probably more power than he realizes. It is difficult for a boss to see the invisible emanations of his own power which accompany his every gesture and word. Power does not feel to the possessor as it looks to others.

The true difference in power between a boss and his subordinate, however, often lies more in the quality of the power than in its absolute quantity. Power comes from several sources. Much of the boss's power accrues to him because of his position and the authority vested in him. It is these sources which essentially confer upon the boss the power to choose, train, evaluate, and even dismiss subordinates (although I believe the firing power of the boss is usually overrated by his subordinates). Generally a subordinate does not have equivalent powers over his boss (though I do know of more than one subordinate who has gotten his boss fired).

[2] Laura Archera Huxley, *You Are Not the Target* (New York: Farrar, Straus & Giroux, 1972).

The boss also tends to control the assignments given to each subordinate, and—despite his pronouncements about the importance of subordinate initiative—rights of initiation belong primarily to the boss. The subordinate can "propose," but it is the boss who "disposes." The subordinate can take initiative, but only within the limits of assignments the boss has given him (or meant to give him).

Another possible source of power for the boss is his knowledge and skill related to the tasks delegated to his subordinates. Here, however, the subordinate is often much more equal and may even have the upper hand. (I wonder if this may not explain why bosses sometimes hold back bits of key information from their subordinates.) If the subordinate is at all competent, he is likely to know more about what he is doing than his boss—if only because the subordinate is actually doing the work, or is one level of supervision closer to whoever is actually doing the work.

As the tasks of an organization become more and more specialized, the power of knowledge and expertise swings more and more to the side of the subordinate. The following rather bizarre example from the defense industry illustrates an extreme case of this shift in power:

Project X was a highly sensitive government scientific-research project. Only the two men working directly on the contract were permitted to have the necessary security clearance to know what the project was about. The boss of the two men found himself theoretically still in charge of them while being denied any knowledge of the project, its progress, or the final results.

Knowledge which the subordinate has can indeed alter his relationship with his boss, because knowledge does confer power. Peter Drucker has pointed out the increasing importance of what he calls the "knowledge worker" or professional specialist. Drucker believes the rise of the career specialist requires a modification of the traditional definition of a boss as someone in command to get results from subordinates; now the crucial role of the manager is more one of responsibility for making a contribution to the organizational goals. Drucker goes on to point out that a career specialist's superior may not be as much his "boss" as he may be a "guide" or "tool" or "marketing arm" upon which the subordinate relies for integration of his output with the needs of the organization and the work of others.[3] (See Chapter 5 for a more thorough exploration of the problems bosses have in dealing with experts or specialists.)

SUBORDINATE STRATEGIES

Differences in power or control help explain why the boss and subordinate often resort to quite different strategies or gambits. The position, authority, and rights of initiation belonging to the boss permit him the use of more offensive strategies, while the subordinate is likely to find defensive or evasive strategies more appropriate. Ducking an assignment by appearing to be unavailable or heavily overloaded, for example, is one common way a subordinate may try to change his boss's plans. The subordinate may delay the progress of a project he does not favor, waiting to see just how hard the boss will push on the project. The subordinate can interpret or execute an assignment in a way that reshapes the original intention of the boss without grossly violating the general meaning of what the boss outlined. If the boss seems to disapprove, the subordinate can always plead a case of legitimate misunderstanding. (Could this be why subordinates sometimes prefer vague directives and purposely do not attempt to clarify what the boss really wants?)

When the subordinate does take the offensive, he finds he cannot openly attack the authority or prerogatives of the boss; the attack must be more indirect, even covert. Managers have no formal mechanism (such as a union) to represent them as subordinates; there are usually no formal procedures through which they can air their grievances (although a few companies are making cautious experiments in both of these directions). As a result, a subordinate may form a temporary coalition with his peers in order to garner enough power to move the boss in a desired direction. Critical incidents or "mini-catastrophes" can also be

[3] Peter F. Drucker, *Management* (New York: Harper & Row, 1974).

an important part of subordinate strategies. These mini-catastrophes can generate concern or attention far beyond what the subordinate himself could create. Some shrewd subordinates who prefer not to wait for critical incidents to arise by themselves develop a real talent for creating controlled catastrophes.

One of the simplest and most potent subordinate gambits involves "withholding"—of information or knowledge or personal effort. Withholding can be an indirect way to strike back or retaliate; that is, the knowledge or effort withheld materially injures the boss or something the boss wants. Sometimes withholding can simply be a way to show the boss that the subordinate does have power (a warning, if you will), to demonstrate just how dependent the boss is on his subordinates.

The key point is that *the choice and use of these defensive and indirect strategies by the subordinate are perfectly natural results of the differences in boss and subordinate powers.*

Unhappily, when the boss stumbles onto one of these subordinate strategies in action, he is likely to become very angry and view the subordinate as obstructive or negative. The boss tends to characterize these subordinate gambits as at best devious and at worst illegitimate. The boss forgets that *he* does not resort to such strategies with his subordinates precisely because he is the boss (although he may indulge in the very same gambits with his own superiors).

WHAT YOU CAN COUNT ON

If bossology includes some things that ain't necessarily so, it also leaves out some things that you can count on.

"The Bigger Picture"

While your boss will tend to know less overall than you think he knows, he is still likely to have some knowledge about your assignments that you do not. The infamous "bigger picture" is what your boss feels he has and wishes you would get. An important part of the bigger picture is all those caveats and constraints the boss is aware of but doesn't state, plus all the other special conditions the boss remembers when you fail to meet them. In one sense the bigger picture is simply a different picture, because your boss's job involves different concerns and activities than yours, different priorities, different groups to be satisfied, different conflicts to be resolved.

Obviously it is to your benefit to learn as much of the bigger picture as you can. But no matter how hard you try, you can never have the "full picture" unless you are literally your own boss. There must always be certain things about which you are not in the know. You must resign yourself to not having the full picture and try to compensate as best you can. For instance, you must continually check out your assumptions, because the odds are some of them are wrong or out-of-date. Such checking does not compromise your intelligence and independence, but is rather an important way to assert these qualities. What *you* don't know (as well as what your boss doesn't know) can hurt you.

Subordinates Are Not the Only Humans

Current bossology stresses the importance of dealing with the human or psychological side of subordinate behavior, but little is said about this aspect of the boss. Doesn't each boss have his own personal package of needs and goals? In fact I suspect there is no more difference between the need packages of a boss and a subordinate than there is between the need packages of two different subordinates or two different bosses. But whatever the assorted needs of the boss, it is his subordinates who must to some degree fulfill those needs (whether or not the subordinates know this, and whether or not they want to).

For instance, as mentioned earlier, a common boss need is to exercise authority and to feel in control. I think of control in two parts: the predictability of something plus the ability to influence that something precisely. If forced to it, I suspect most bosses would happily settle for just the predictability part of control. In more colloquial terms, most bosses don't want surprises.

At the very minimum, a boss would like to feel he controls his subordinates. So, as a subordinate, if you are going to try something new or deviate from your normal pattern, you are well advised to give your boss plenty of warning. The more independent you seem, the more you may threaten the boss's feeling of authority and control over you (even if the boss generally likes what you do on your own). But *letting your boss know what you are up to is not the same thing as asking permission for everything.* "Touching base" with the boss gives him the feeling he could modify what you are doing, if he wanted to. Just like investment prospectuses, it is amazing what you can get away with if you just disclose what you are doing.

The typical boss also likes to feel that his subordinates are dependent on him to some degree. If you "do it all," then your boss may get to wondering what he is there for. Bosses like to feel needed—as long as this doesn't require dealing with too many sticky problems. Subordinates can apply participative management to their bosses as well as the other way around. Find out the kind of inputs your boss likes to make and give him some chance to do what he likes. This way *you* can decide when and where the boss's input will be most helpful (or least harmful), and your boss may be more inclined to leave you alone in other areas.

There is even nothing wrong with confessing ignorance or appearing helpless every now and then, although some subordinates overuse this gambit. On the other hand, don't ask your boss for his opinion or help just for the sake of appearances. Your boss may feel compelled to give you an opinion even when he doesn't have one.

Believe it or not, bosses also want to be liked, even admired. You may spend relatively little time with your boss, but he may be spending the majority of his working day with his subordinates. It can be pretty depressing for a boss to spend most of his day with people who he feels do not like him, or who are at best neutral. Igor Radović, in his book on how to manage one's boss, makes this cynical observation:

> *The superior . . . craves positive recognition* more than most people. *To get it, he depends heavily on the subordinate* (it being

seldom likely that recognition will come from any other quarter), *and is willing and ready to pay a good price for it.*[4]

When your boss does something you like or admire, it doesn't hurt to let him know your positive feelings. Temporarily withdrawing your "liking" also can be a very powerful tool in your repertory. Of course, the use of these emotional gambits depends on your having a decent relationship with your boss in the first place.

In short, *don't get trapped into responding only to the "managerial" side of your boss,* even though that may sound like what he wants. Some bosses couch everything in terms of the job, without ever openly admitting the importance of their own personal goals. When you catch your boss playing some "games" you dislike, don't condemn him out of hand. You are not the only one struggling to fulfill your personal desires.

Your Personal Goals Are Subordinate

An enlightened boss may be aware of your personal needs and even tend to them from time to time, but they are rarely his major concern. No matter how you slice it, you are hired primarily to fulfill certain organizational needs. If you do not adequately perform your job, then both you and your boss are in trouble; the fact that you (perhaps aided by your boss) are getting all sorts of personal satisfactions will do little to mitigate the trouble.

Of course, for you the priorities are just the opposite. You will be understandably upset if your personal goals are not being satisfactorily achieved, and the fact that you are doing good work on the job may do little to make up for it. Incidentally, the discrepancy between organizational and personal goals is usually greater the further down the organization you look.

Thus subordinates tend to see their bosses as evil, immoral, or just plain uncaring because they do not proffer much aid in fulfilling the personal goals of subordinates. But remember, your boss is continually juggling the organization's goals, his personal

[4] Igor Radović, *The Radović Rule* (New York: M. Evans & Co., 1973).

needs, and your personal desires. The fact that *you are not his only subordinate* only adds to the difficulty of his juggling act. Moreover, many of the things subordinates want are in short supply: money, prestige, power, promotion, recognition. Even when these things are not so scarce, each subordinate wants to have more than other subordinates. So the odds are that most subordinates will not get most of what they want.

Naturally, organizational and personal goals will overlap to some degree (otherwise the organization will not survive long). To a large degree, however, responsibility for satisfying your personal goals is yours, not yours boss's. It is basically up to you to make your goals known (if appropriate); to apply your ingenuity toward fulfilling them; to do battle for them when necessary; and to chose among the inevitable compromises you will have to make between what you want (including what you want for the organization as well as for yourself) and what the organization or your boss wants.

There's No Thrill in Getting What's Expected

Every once in a while I happen to be talking with a manager in his office when he receives his pay envelope. The ritual is almost always the same. The manager calmly opens the envelope, usually without missing a beat of the conversation. He quietly glances at the amount of the check and stuffs it away in his pocket or a desk drawer. The manager's face does not flush with gratitude. He does not rush off to thank his boss or offer me a quick drink to celebrate. He simply goes on about his business. The manager has received what was expected, for performing the tasks assigned.

The boss regards your work performance in much the same way. Every week or month you perform certain assigned tasks, and let us assume you do the work quite competently. You are doing what is expected, what you are paid to do. Yet you would like to receive some special recognition from the boss once in a while, even if it is only a word of thanks or praise. You feel that not all subordinates are really competent; jobs often do not get done for a variety of reasons. You are probably right, but competence and getting the job done are still what your boss *expects,* no matter how rare such occurrences may actually be.

Our expectations represent a sort of zero point. When our expectations are not met, a negative score rings up on our internal tote board; we feel disappointed or distressed. When our expectations are met, no score rings up; we feel neutral. When our expectations are exceeded, a positive score rings up; lights may flash, and we feel excited and pleased.

Just doing a good job on what was assigned rings up a "no score" on your boss's tote board (unless of course he thinks you are a dolt and is amazed to find you did something right for a change). *To really "score" with your boss, you have to do something he did not expect* (but something he wanted). Even if you have to slight a few less-important parts of your normal job to do this "something extra," your overall score may still register very high.

Surprising your boss, of course, does involve some risk: The something extra may turn out to be something the boss did not want. In a curious way, then, it turns out that subordinates are rewarded for successful risk-taking just as bosses are.

Feedback Is Always Available If You Want It

Bossology harps on the importance of providing feedback to subordinates. Strange to say, bosses generally do provide plenty of feedback, but not always in the fashion implied by bossology. Your boss is human, and that means he has a continuing stream of reactions to you and what you do. Unless your boss is a consummate actor, he will inevitably manifest many of those reactions. Such reactions, however, will not necessarily take the form of an explicit, verbal appraisal of how you are doing. Indeed, most bosses are not very skilled in providing formal feedback, and approach a quarterly or annual appraisal meeting with as much fear and trembling as the subordinate. Anyway, such formal appraisal sessions usually occur far too long after the fact to be really useful to either party.

The constant stream of feedback is there, but the responsibility for hearing or seeing the feedback is primarily yours.

First, you really have to want the feedback. Many of us say we want feedback when what we really mean is *we want favorable feedback*. Next, you have to learn how to read your boss's reactions. What kind of nonverbal communication does your boss give you when you discuss an assignment: Is he fidgeting, impatient, serious, reflective? What is his tone of voice? What does your boss kid you about? Joking is often a way of indirectly expressing concerns too touchy to talk about directly. How much time does your boss spend with you? What does he do with your ideas? Does he tell you they're wonderful and then take no action on them, or does he say nothing but proceed to quietly adopt (or even steal) some of them?

Such informal or indirect feedback can be tricky to interpret. If the boss rejects four out of five of your ideas, you may feel disheartened. On the other hand, the boss may be very pleased overall that you came up with the one good idea he accepted. A smile or a scowl can have many meanings, and may not even be specifically directed at or caused by you. Still, nothing stops you from tactfully testing out your feedback interpretations from time to time. For instance if your boss says something more or less positive in what you fear is a weak-sounding way, you might say something like, "You don't sound convinced" or "I gather you're not really happy about this thing, right?"

If you want to encourage more explicit feedback from your boss, it is important that you *do not overreact to either praise or criticism*. If you are pleased by something the boss says about you, it doesn't hurt to say so, but don't make it sound as if you now feel you're the greatest thing since the computer. If you're unhappy about what your boss has just said about you, the less you say about your reactions the better. Make sure you fully understand what your boss has said, but avoid plunging into an ardent defense of yourself; don't try to make him change his opinion right there on the spot. Above all, do not argue with your boss about his evaluation (at least for the moment) or you will greatly inhibit him from providing much direct feedback in the future. If you want to throw a fit, or do some brooding, or plot your defense, retire first to the privacy of your own office.

To repeat: Feedback is always available, but you have to want it!

Don't Bet on Changing Your Boss

How often have you felt that if only the boss would do a few little things differently, the effect would be enormous? Unfortunately, grousing about your boss or wishing he were different won't make him change. It may even be difficult to think of any *action* you could take that would make him change.

On the other hand, there are usually several things you can change (other than your boss) that would improve the situation. However, upon contemplating these changes, you may judge they will have nowhere near the impact of the changes you wish your boss would make. You may feel so discouraged by the small impact you're capable of having that you fruitlessly continue to ponder (or complain about) what the boss is doing wrong.

At this point I direct your attention to a somewhat immodestly titled "law" which may lead you to see things in a slightly different light:

GOLDE'S LAW

The expected value of changing your boss is generally less than the expected value of changing yourself.

Let me explain. "Expected value" is a concept used in the field of probability and is simply a kind of weighted judgment that reflects *both* the size of a payoff and the chances of actually getting the payoff (by multiplying them together). For example, if you play a state lottery (with, say, 2 million tickets outstanding), the payoff may be very large (say, $1 million), but the odds of winning are very low (1 in 2,000,000, to be exact). The expected value of your lottery ticket would be the $1 million payoff multiplied by your 1-in-2,000,000 chance of winning (.0000005) —a total of 50¢, which is probably less than what you would have to pay for the ticket.

Golde's Law applies the same weighted-value approach as a way of comparing the options of changing your boss versus changing yourself. The *effects* of changing yourself are smaller than the effects of changing your boss, but the *chances* of changing yourself are much higher than for changing your boss (although changing yourself is by no means easy). Golde's Law claims that the higher odds of changing yourself usually outweigh the smaller effects of changing yourself. In short, you are better off betting on yourself than on your boss.

THE SUBORDINATE SITUATION

Take Care of Your Boss! The Next One May Be Worse

As subordinates we sometimes find a certain solace in accepting the view of the boss as the "superior," which of course leaves us as the "inferior." Yet for the most part we do not really believe that being subordinate means being inferior. Bossology creates the presumption that bosses manage and take care of their subordinates, whereas in reality the reverse is often just as true: An effective, successful subordinate will manage and take care of his boss. Incidentally, the way we care for our boss can significantly affect the way our subordinates care for and judge *us*.

Deep down we all know that bosses have human needs and human failings; that bosses have their own battles and burdens; that much of the fault we find in bosses is caused by matters outside their control; that bosses are not so different from subordinates; that on the average we can only expect bosses to be average. We may know all this, but we often find it more convenient to act as if we didn't, because *doing so can relieve us of responsibilities we might prefer not to shoulder*.

We must be careful not to confuse what we would like with what we can legitimately expect. If we expect our bosses to be the mythical managers portrayed in bossology, we doom ourselves (and quite probably our bosses) to constant disappointment and frustration. We must expect the boss to have important shortcomings for which in large measure we, as subordinates, will have to compensate.

So on those rare occasions when the boss in fact does something right, we ought to feel pleased or even grateful instead of feeling, "It's about time." Every now and then we might even startle the boss by offering him a word of encouragement or thanks.

Expose Yourself

If as a subordinate you are not necessarily inferior, you are also not necessarily very visible. You are only one of a number of subordinates doing the work you are assigned. One way to become more visible is to excel, but you must also ensure that appropriate data and measurements are available to demonstrate your excellence. Another approach for gaining visibility that was already mentioned is to do something extra, something other than the tasks you are assigned. Participation in certain extracurricular activities can also be a way to increase your visibility—for example, writing a magazine article, speaking at public or community functions, or working with an appropriate trade association.

"Differentiation" is yet another strategy for achieving visibility.

A young man was hired to work in the mailroom of a large automobile-manufacturing company. He noticed that all the mailroom employees dressed rather casually, so he decided to differentiate himself by always wearing a coat and tie. The young man quickly became quite visible and was soon promoted out of the mailroom to more interesting work.

Differentiation can take many forms besides the way you dress —for example, the style of your memos, your work habits, what you do at meetings, how you arrange your office. There is, however, an important distinction to be noted between differentiation and eccentricity. The latter behavior is usually tolerated only among very senior managers, if at all.

The Ultimate Weapon

You can try to change your boss or others in the organization; you can change yourself to some degree or make new compromises between what you want and what you are willing to live with. But even you can change or compromise only so much. Substantially improving an unhappy situation may still not make it tolerable. You (and your boss as well) control only a few of the many factors responsible for your job dissatisfaction. Your boss may indeed be hopelessly incompetent, power mad, or frighteningly paranoid. Your department may be irrevocably out of political favor with the powers that be. Your projects may in fact be incurably boring, unrealistically conceived, or unavoidably doomed to failure.

Just as your boss's ultimate weapon is his capacity to fire you, so *your ultimate weapon is the ability to leave the job* (which, when you think about it, is actually a way to fire your boss). But *the ultimate weapon has no power unless you are willing to use it.* It is difficult to bluff your willingness to leave; your true state of mind will show through. The key to how willing you are to leave is simply your knowledge of other job offers or your confidence that you can find them if need be.

Certainly you can abuse this ultimate weapon by threatening to quit every time something does not go your way. Certainly there is some risk in seeking out other job opportunities. Nobody is indispensable, and your boss can feel you are "disloyal" if he finds out you are looking around. But your boss is just as likely to interpret your other job offers as a sign of your capability; after all, if someone else wants you, then perhaps you're worth more than he thought. At least the boss may take you less for granted. The very knowledge that you do have other options can also help you develop a more positive attitude toward the job you presently hold.

Sure, you can be tagged as a "job hopper" if you switch jobs too often. But nowadays most companies are less concerned than they used to be about hiring someone who has changed jobs a few times. In fact, some organizations even prefer to hire managers with experience in several different organizations or types of work. Moreover, staying in any one job too long may "typecast" you in a way that makes it difficult to acquire broader responsibilities. Also, the salary increase that accompanies a job change is often much greater than you could expect from remaining with your own company for several years.

Far from overusing the ultimate weapon, many subordinates seem to ignore its very existence. Yet your willingness to quit is the fundamental power you have—the power on which most of your other powers depend, the power which (whether you like it or not) underlies all your negotiations about pay, status, assignments, and your future. The reality is that *no matter who you're working for, you're on your own payroll.*

3:
DISCRETION:
Do It My Way on Your Own

THE SEARCH FOR RISKLESS FREEDOM

They were having lunch in a sandwich shop, but the same conversation could have occurred over the water cooler or during a coffee break.

STAN: So anyway, I *finally* get in to see my boss about this report I'm doing on the new branch and all he does is chew me out because I talked to some town officials to get some information I needed.

STEVE: Yeah, I know what you mean. My boss just can't delegate anything either. Like this SR project. I'm trying to do what I think is best, but whatever I come up with he blows his stack at it because it isn't what he wanted.

STAN: Right. I need some authority to handle the things that keep popping up. I can't keep checking with him; he's not even *there* half the time.

Meanwhile, around the corner, their bosses are also talking.

BILL: Damn right I'm upset. I gave Stan this new branch plan to work on and he comes in today with a real mish-mash.

> The only concrete thing he'd done was to stir up the city officials, and you know what a can of worms that is. Then Stan wonders why I try to keep tabs on him.

BEN: Well, I get the same kind of problem. Steve and I spent a lot of time reaching agreement about what we need on this SR project, but he keeps sticking his head in the door three times a day to check. I wish he'd just go off and get the thing done.

BILL: Absolutely. I wish Stan would surprise me just once: figure out what's needed, put it all together—on time, ready to go—and bring it to me for approval.

It's a rare day indeed when the topic of discretion does not in some way drift into these daily, informal conversations. Yet people's attitudes about discretion are a very curious collection. Subordinates want more of it, bosses feel subordinates don't use it when they have it, and I believe subordinates are usually given too much of it. Vague assignments confer a lot of it, yet subordinates complain about such vagueness; bosses often complain when subordinates actually use it. Yet, despite all this confusion, bosses and subordinates rarely talk to each other directly about it.

The role of discretion is crucial to the never-ending drama of how jobs are assigned and carried out and of how bosses and subordinates work together to fulfill organizational and personal needs. The growing concern about making life on the job more satisfying simply gives discretion an extra shove toward center-stage.

The Duality of Discretion

I was startled one day to realize that the very word "discretion" has a double meaning that immediately discloses a part of the dilemma. On the one hand, the dictionary defines discretion as the freedom and authority to make decisions and choices, the power to judge or act as one wishes. On the other hand, the second meaning of discretion is the quality of being discreet or careful about what one does and says; prudence. So the word discretion contains both the notion of independence or freedom and the notion of safety or security. The struggle to integrate these two diverse meanings of discretion is a very central issue in most boss-subordinate relationships.

The boss and subordinate usually agree (more or less) on the desirability of independence and freedom for the subordinate. They also usually agree that security for each of them depends, at least in part, on having things turn out the way the boss wants. From here on out, things are not quite so agreeable.

DISCRETION DOUBLE-THINK

In general, the more independence a boss gives his subordinate (or the more independence a subordinate exercises), the greater the risk that things will not turn out as the boss wants. However, if both the boss and subordinate are smart managers, they will try to minimize risk-taking, which is hard to do without compromising the subordinate's freedom. The attempts of both boss and subordinate to "have their cake and eat it too" usually result in a kind of double-think (or double-talk if you will).

"Do it my way on your own" is what the subordinate tends to "hear" from his boss, or alternatively, "Do what I want without my having to ask." The bind is as obvious as it is inescapable. If the subordinate does it "on his own" or "without asking," he incurs a substantial risk of not doing what the boss wants. To make sure the boss gets what he wants, the subordinate may end up doing it less on his own than either he or his boss might like.

What the boss tends to "hear" from his subordinate is "Help me do it myself," or alternatively, "Don't be upset if I try something on my own that doesn't work out." The subordinate wants the boss to accept whatever happens. What's the poor boss to do? If he helps the subordinate, then the subordinate has not done it by himself. But how can a boss guarantee approval of whatever the subordinate does; how can he agree not to be upset if the subordinate makes a serious mistake?

Both the boss and the subordinate are searching for riskless freedom, and it is this quest which creates such paradoxical attitudes: Subordinates may desire more discretion (freedom) but not always use the discretion they have (for security's sake);

bosses often confer discretion (freedom) but complain when the discretion is exercised (because it violates their security).

Delegation Dogma

The term "discretion" itself does not appear very often in the management literature. The security and freedom issues, however, are treated to some degree under such interrelated rubrics as delegation, management by exception, management by objectives (MBO), and participative management. For the sake of convenience I will refer to the general combination of all these topics as "the standard approach to delegation."

The usual description of effective delegation goes something like this:

> The achievement by a manager of definite, specified results by providing subordinates with the widest possible latitude for the accomplishment of all or part of the specific results for which the manager has final accountability.[1]

Such a description is typically followed by a discussion of how the subordinate needs to have the necessary authority to make decisions and take actions to achieve the desired result. As a corollary it is pointed out that after conferring the proper authority on the subordinate, the boss should stay out of the subordinate's hair. The subordinate should be left alone to direct and manage his own efforts, subject of course to some sort of periodic checks on his progress.

Thus, in the standard approach, delegation tries to ensure that things turn out the way the boss wants (the security factor) through careful definition of end results. Delegation provides independence and freedom for the subordinate by giving him full responsibility for taking appropriate action to achieve the specified results.

Management by exception essentially says that as long as things are going okay, the boss should not interfere. Reports and other procedures are set up to generate red flags that signal when

[1] Dale D. McConkey, *No-Nonsense Delegation* (New York: AMACOM, 1974).

something may be wrong. The "exception" technique presumably provides maximum independence for the subordinate yet provides the boss with some way to assure himself that when things don't proceed as he desires, he will know about it.

MBO emphasizes that it is important to clearly define tasks when one is delegating work. MBO stresses that objectives should be stated as specifically as possible, in terms of results rather than activities. MBO also focuses on the need to determine meaningful ways to measure results, so that progress toward objectives can be evaluated.

Participative management, which links into MBO, emphasizes the importance of having subordinates participate in the actual development or acceptance of the objectives which are subsequently assigned to them. The hope is that subordinate participation in goal-setting will provide them with a clearer idea of exactly what is desired as well as a greater commitment to achieving the goal. The advocates of participative management also stress that the very process of participation can itself help fulfill subordinates' desires for independence and self-realization.

What intrigues me is that the standard approach to delegation has become more than merely a set of possibly useful managerial tools; it has become a model of how managers ought to behave to minimize the dilemma of discretion. The model is so neat and reasonable that we have implicitly assumed it fits the real world of organizations. The model is sufficiently seductive that any problems encountered tend to be attributed to some failure in correctly applying the techniques. Perhaps the objective was simply not made specific enough; or the subordinate just did not clearly understand the objective; or the objective was arbitrarily imposed on the subordinate; or the boss does not sufficiently trust his subordinate; or the subordinate really doesn't have good judgment; or the objective should have included qualitative as well as quantitative factors; or the reporting system should be fixed to pick up the data needed for performance measurement.

I admit that many MBO systems are poorly installed, badly introduced, or not complete enough. I agree that managers often lack the skills necessary to make the system work and that sometimes managers even hold attitudes unconducive to the proper functioning of the model. I applaud attempts to improve or patch the system, to educate managers in the necessary skills, or to provide incentives that will change the attitudes of people hostile to the system. What troubles me is the lack of any attempt to take a hard look at the model itself, to see whether it really is a meaningful ideal to shoot for. In other words, *problems that crop up are consistently attributed to failures of implementation rather than to deficiencies in the model.*

This unquestioning acceptance of the model is clearly illustrated by the comment of a manager whose company had just scrapped its formal MBO system:

> There is still no question in my mind about the importance of setting clear objectives so I can give my subordinates full responsibility for getting things done. I just think our MBO system resulted in a lot of extra paperwork and fancy meetings that really didn't get to the heart of the matter.

Now, I can't definitively prove that something important is missing from the standard approach to delegation. Few formal measurements have been made of the effectiveness of delegation or related programs. (Ironic, isn't it, that most MBO programs do not establish any specific objectives and measurements for the MBO program itself?)

My suspicions about the delegation model are fanned by taking a hard look at some of the problems managers describe with regard to the standard techniques of delegation (even while embracing them as some kind of ideal):

> You know, it's awfully hard to really pin down a lot of things, especially when complex jobs are involved and you never know exactly what you're going to get into.

> Sometimes organizationwide objectives just don't fit the situation in our area.

> You know, the problem is that objectives are all interrelated and there can also be a lot of conflict between organizational and personal goals.

This measurement and progress thing is what bugs me. It's hard to nail everything down in numbers, and when you use something else a lot of personal judgment and interpretation are involved. Besides, a lot of the time, things work out or not due to factors that are really outside your control.

Of course you can interpret these comments as simply additional instances of failure to properly implement the standard delegation model. But a hard look at these statements also suggests certain incongruities between the real world of management and the world assumed by the standard approach to delegation. In particular, *objectives* in the real world of organizations may not have the characteristics assumed by the standard theory of delegation. The rest of this chapter develops what I think these managers are sensing, and what the implications of such observations may be.

OBJECTIVES ARE SELDOM WHAT THEY SEEM

Terms such as "needs," "goals," and "programs" are sometimes used to mean the same thing as "objectives." These terms may take on various different meanings, with the distinctions differing from organization to organization. For the moment I want to avoid worrying about the possible distinctions among these terms, and so I will use the word "objectives" in a broad, general way to refer to what an organization, boss, or subordinate wants (which is often specified in the assignment of a job or task).

The literature and seminars on delegation, MBO, and so forth, repeat over and over again the following kinds of statements about objectives:

1. Objectives should be *specific;* i.e., clear and unambiguous.
2. Objectives should be *complete,* fully specifying what is desired.
3. Objectives represent "ends"; they should be separated and distinguished from "means" for attaining the objectives.
4. Objectives should be stated in terms that permit measurement of progress toward them.

Now, each of these statements or recommendations is in reality based on a very important but usually unspoken assumption. Take the first statement. If you state that "objectives *should* be specific," you are implicitly assuming that objectives *can* be specific. Substituting the words "can be" for "should be" in each of the other statements also produces a key assumption whose validity, I believe, is open to some question. I propose to examine the assumptions behind each of the first three statements in order to see how these assumptions hold up in the real world of the manager. (If these first three assumptions do not hold up, then there will be no need to deal specifically with the fourth assumption about the measurability of objectives. That is, if objectives cannot really be specific, complete, and distinguished from "means," then it is rather unreasonable to assume that they can generally be stated in terms that permit measurement of progress toward them.)

Specificity, or "A Collection of Holes"

Here is a memo (only slightly condensed) that was sent out by the headquarters of a major manufacturer of office equipment.

> To: All District Sales Managers
> From: Vice President/Sales
> Subject: Improving the quality of Customer Contacts
>
> As you all know, we are experiencing a disturbing decline in repeat business from our major accounts. As part of our overall effort to improve this situation, we are instituting the following program which should be put into effect immediately:
>
> 1. All District Managers should spend at least 40 percent of their time accompanying salesmen on customer calls.
>
> 2. All key customers representing annual sales of $70,000 or more should be called on by a salesman at least once a quarter and contacted by phone at least once a month.
>
> 3. Each District Sales Manager should personally contact each account where sales have dropped 25 percent or more from last year.

Let us not argue whether the objectives outlined in the above memo are the right ones to remedy the problem. The point is that by many standards, the objectives set forth do seem to be reasonably specific and precise. Some of the objectives are even pinned down in terms of easily measured numbers—frequency of calls, dollar volumes, percentage declines, and so on. Yet here is a sample of the typical way this memo was greeted in the field:

SAM: Well, I guess we've got the word now. All we have to do is figure out what it means. Like what does 40 percent of my time mean? Is it 40 percent of the time I spend in the field or 40 percent of all my time? Is it 40 percent on the average or every month or what?

TOM: Look, whichever way you slice it, I don't see how I'm supposed to do all this extra work without more help. And who's going to cover for me at the office? Frankly, our problem isn't too little time on the road, it's too little homework to make our calls productive.

SAM: Yeah, and it's ridiculous to bother an account every month if they're already giving us all their business. Besides, how am I supposed to know if a *new* account is "key" or not until they actually buy?

TOM: Right. Also, I think I ought to be spending my time on the tough accounts, which aren't necessarily the large ones. And what am I supposed to *do* when I visit an account with my salesman? That's the real question. This memo is just a collection of holes.

SAM: Well, I suppose I don't mind the holes so much except that we've got to do the clarifying. The only trouble is, those birds in the head office just don't realize it.

Certainly the vice president of sales could have clarified a few of the points and covered a few of the more likely contingencies. But it would take a 50-page manual to try and cover everything, and even then there would no doubt still be quite a few holes. The thick procedure manuals compiled by many government agencies or large business organizations can never quite seem to plug all the gaps.

One trouble is that the further from the scene of action a manager is, the more difficult it is for him to know what really needs pinning down. Moreover, local situations do vary a great deal. Any attempt by headquarters to spell out exact details would be wasted (i.e., not applicable across the board). Even the local sales manager on the firing line could not state all the vital details without first spending some time trying to carry out the new directives.

Sometimes it may actually be desirable for objectives not to be fully specific. Frequently, different groups involved in a task will have varying viewpoints about what the organization's goals should be, and personal goals will conflict with organizational goals. If an exact, precise consensus on a goal or its meaning were required before any action were taken, the operation of most American organizations would come to a standstill.

An objective that did represent the ultimate in specificity would in essence have to be a set of detailed instructions to be mechanically carried out, with no possibility of any discretion. But we need not worry; the impreciseness of language (not to mention other factors) is sufficient to guarantee failure in the achievement of ultimate specificity. In the real world of managers, objectives are always stated at a somewhat general or abstract level. They are always somewhat ambiguous and open to alternative interpretations. To some degree an objective is always "a collection of holes"—at least, this seems like a more realistic assumption on which to base an approach to the delegation problem.

Completeness, or Half a Whole Ball of Wax

A Midwestern manufacturer of plastic consumer products was about to negotiate an annual purchase contract for many thousand pounds of a key raw material. The firm (I'll call it Playfab) was experiencing a relatively severe cost-price squeeze, and the purchasing objective was about as simple and apparently self-contained as any you could find:

We want competitive bids on this supply contract and we will go with the lowest bidders, though in no case will we pay more than $3 a pound.

Of course you will have noticed that this objective has some holes in it similar to those discussed in the preceding section. For example, do payment terms affect the price that Playfab is willing to pay? How many competitive bids are required? And how do shipping and insurance costs fit into the price per pound? But in this case, I don't want to pursue the holes. Rather, I want to focus on a whole set of other, related objectives—objectives which constitute firm company policy regarding purchase contracts but which are not mentioned in the statement cited above. For instance, Playfab's policies include the following:

1. Suppliers must be noncompetitive (i.e., not supply Playfab competitors).
2. Suppliers must be nonreciprocal (i.e., not customers of Playfab).
3. Suppliers must be equal opportunity employers.
4. Suppliers must run "union shops."
5. Preference is given to suppliers qualifying as "small businesses."
6. No more than 30 percent of any one material is to be purchased from a single supplier.
7. Suppliers must meet certain quality specifications.
8. Suppliers must agree to certain packing specifications.
9. Suppliers must appear competent to meet a rigid delivery schedule.
10. Suppliers must be "financially stable," as determined by ground rules set out by the controller's department.

Clearly, the initial statement of the objective was incomplete as it stood. The problem was that some of the ten related objectives (or constraints, if you will) were stated in writing and some were not. Some of the ten objectives were of long standing and relatively well known and some were not (in fact, some of the additional policies were still being strongly protested). There was no single place at Playfab where all ten of the additional conditions were collectively stated.

The incompleteness found in Playfab's statement of a purchasing objective is more the rule than the exception. If anything, the surrounding, unstated objectives are usually even less well-defined. Professor Herbert Simon describes the general situation like this:

> In the decision-making situations of real life, a course of action, to be acceptable, must satisfy a whole set of requirements, or constraints. Sometimes one of these requirements is singled out and referred to as the goal of the action. But the choice of one of the constraints from many is to a large extent arbitrary. . . . Those constraints that motivate the decision maker and those that guide his search for actions are sometimes regarded as more "goal-like" than those that limit the actions he may consider or those that are used to test whether a potential course of action he has designed is satisfactory.[2]

In other words, Playfab should not be criticized for omitting the additional constraints or objectives that made up the "whole ball of wax." Playfab quite reasonably relied on the general knowledge of the purchasing department to include all the missing policies. Obviously, *it is very easy for one of those unspoken or unlisted objectives to be overlooked,* and in many cases *there may in fact be considerable disagreement as to exactly what the unmentioned constraints really are.*

A very famous example of such problems occurred during the Cuban missile crisis. President John F. Kennedy ordered the navy to set up a blockade. The navy interpreted the order as giving it license to practice anti-submarine-warfare procedures which it had been developing. The navy's actions, however, ran entirely contrary to the intent of the blockade ordered by the President.

Differences between the spirit and the letter of the law result in much the same set of problems. The letter of the law is exactly what the law expressly states. The spirit of the law contains all

[2] Herbert Simon, "On the Concept of Organization Goal," *Administrative Science Quarterly* (June 1964).

the other implied but unstated conditions, caveats, and constraints. A more folksy saying points up the same problem in another way: "Be careful what you wish for; you might get it." Any wish you make contains a vast, unstated context that goes along with it. You may get your wish (to the letter), but it may be fulfilled in a wholly different context (spirit) than you desired but did not state. The effect of that wholly different context may completely subvert the original intention of your wish. Midas asked for the golden touch and was given it, but he hadn't expected a touch that was all *that* golden.

To paraphrase: "Be careful what you ask of your subordinate (or boss); he might do it."

The Hierarchy of Ends (or Is It Means?)

The desires of any organization can be pictured as a ladder with many rungs—each rung from the top down representing a more specific level of desires. The terms used to identify each rung of the ladder vary from organization to organization, and sometimes vary even within the same organization. These variances in termi-

nology often create considerable confusion, but I am less interested in resolving semantic disputes than in examining the relationships among the rungs on the ladder, whatever they may be called. A typical ladder (with arbitrarily selected terms to identify the rungs) might look like this:

Values (desire for the company to be an industry leader and produce something of true value to the customer)
Goals (e.g., "a chicken in every pot")
Objectives (e.g., 15 percent growth per year)
Policies (e.g., expand sales coverage to every major U.S. city)
Programs (e.g., open Midwestern sales office)
Tasks (e.g., find sales manager for Midwestern sales office)

I should point out that in most organizations there is considerable uncertainty and disagreement about the contents of the top rung, which more or less represents the ultimate purposes of life. So the top rung is usually not talked about very explicitly.

Charles Granger, a management consultant, has called this kind of ladder a "hierarchy of objectives," and he defines objectives in the relatively broad, everyday sense of management language as: "an aim or end of action." [3] But is opening up a new sales office in the Midwest an end of action or simply part of the means to achieve the objective of expanding sales coverage to every major U.S. city? Is expanding sales coverage the real objective or merely a means for increasing growth?

I submit that an organization's hierarchy of objectives (or ends) may equally well be looked at as a hierarchy of *means*. Any one rung of the ladder (or hierarchy) is in one sense a means—a means for reaching a higher rung of the ladder. At the same time, each rung of the ladder is an "end"—an end to be attained by means of the lower rungs on the ladder. Each rung (except the top one) is both a means *and* an end, depending on whether you look up or down the ladder from there. So the difference between means and ends turns out to be *a point of view*

---

[3] Charles H. Granger, "The Hierarchy of Objectives," *Harvard Business Review* (May–June 1964).

rather than some intrinsic characteristic of a particular action, decision, or statement.

The interrelationship of the various rungs helps explain why it is highly unlikely that any one rung will be fully specific and complete. Each rung of the ladder somewhat determines and influences the rungs below it; conversely, the lower rungs define and complete the rungs of the ladder above. Of course the picture is further complicated in real life, because there are typically several criss-crossed ladders of objectives representing the objectives of different groups and varying personal interests.

All of this is by way of explaining what most managers already know: the way a subordinate carries out a task can completely alter (intentionally or not) the original objective of the task. For example, quotas or budgets represent relatively specific and complete objectives, but the quota has not yet been devised that cannot be "beaten," as in the following anecdote:

The monthly production quota for a screw manufacturing plant was sharply increased—beyond the capacity of the equipment. Since the number of screws produced is cumbersome to determine, all quotas were stated in terms of weight. So the astute plant manager simply modified the mixture of raw materials used in order to increase the weight of each screw produced, and went on producing the old number of screws.

How Does the Boss Know What He Wants Until He Sees What's Been Done?

Up to here we have been talking about the assumptions that objectives can be stated specifically and completely and can be separated from the means for achieving them. But there is an even more fundamental assumption that needs questioning—namely, that objectives can always be stated. In the previous chapter I suggested that the boss (or the organization) doesn't always know what he (or it) wants. Obviously, if the boss doesn't know exactly what he wants, he may have some trouble describing his desires.

I am not talking about a boss who is simply lazy or who doesn't do the appropriate homework to sort out his thoughts.

Management problems don't always come in neat packages, and even neat packages may be very complicated. Sometimes the real problems are not very evident; all the boss knows about is a collection of symptoms. And sometimes the symptoms are not even clear—the boss just smells trouble somewhere. Problem-finding is as time-consuming and important a management task as problem-solving.

Consider the example of the marketing vice president of a medium-sized metal products manufacturer who called in Ernie (one of his managers) to give him a new assignment and explained it this way:

> You know how our top executives have been getting all these complaint calls, and our sales managers just don't have the time to handle all the problems. Now, as part of our program to improve customer service, our Executive Committee has decided to set up a new customer-relations function. Ernie, we want you to take charge of this new group, which will function as a liaison with all the operating divisions.
>
> The job needs someone who really knows our business and someone who's a good manager, but who also knows how to be diplomatic with the customers. We think you're the kind of guy who can take charge and get results quickly. You know how vital this area is, with all the competition out there ready to pounce on our mistakes.

Feeling pleased, Ernie went off to set about his new job. The assignment seemed clear enough, and it seemed to be one in which his success (or lack of it) would be fairly evident.

Within a few weeks Ernie became a rather confused and dejected manager. The salesmen said the problems were in accounting; the accountants said the plant was causing all the trouble; the production people blamed both purchasing and engineering. Ernie found he didn't know whether he was supposed to do just a good job of "hand-holding" with the customer or track down the real cause of a complaint. Was he supposed to report the complaint to the appropriate department, or should he actually take steps to see that the source of the problem was corrected in the future? Was he going to be judged on the basis of how many complaints he handled effectively, or how many problems he uncovered, or how many problems he fixed for the future? In fact, with all the special attention he and his group were paying to complaints, the actual number of complaints might even increase.

Ernie decided to go back to his boss for some clarification of objectives. What he got was a lot more straight-from-the-shoulder generalities. The boss kept saying, "Delighted you're taking hold. Just keep the customers happy. Let me know anytime you have a problem. My door is always open."

You can argue that the boss was simply unwilling to think things through and dropped Ernie in the middle, hoping he would be able to thrash his way out. I find it just as reasonable to suppose that Ernie's boss didn't have enough information to clarify the job any more than this—that what the boss really wanted was for Ernie to find out exactly what was wrong and what needed doing, and then to take appropriate action (all without stepping on anyone's toes, of course). After all, isn't that what subordinate managers are there for?

Well, Ernie finally did arrive at some conclusions about what to do and took some positive action. The next thing he knew, his boss hauled him up short. It seems the boss was getting a lot of complaints about the Complaint Group; Ernie had stirred up trouble, and besides, the customer complaints were still flowing in. Ernie left the session muttering about how his boss always changes the signals on him.

Another case of poor delegation was recorded in that great managerial account book in the sky.

LET'S FACE THE FUZZ

Discretion Doesn't Feel Like It Looks

In the discretion of others, we see freedom. In the discretion we have (or confer), we find risk and lack of security. In the discretion we dream of, we imagine riskless freedom. The standard model of delegation beckons forth as the fulfillment of our dream

—precise, clear objectives to minimize the risk, and choice of methods to provide the freedom. We rush to embrace MBO, management by exception, participative management, and the other techniques only to find that risk and lack of security are not so easily banished.

To put it in one word, the nature of objectives is "fuzzy," and the higher up in the organization you look, the fuzzier the objectives become. The whole act of having someone else do something for you is fraught with fuzziness: It is difficult to know exactly what you want and at least as hard to describe what you want specifically or completely enough to serve as an unambiguous guide to action. You may not know, really, how you want the objective carried out or whether the other person can actually handle it, and in many cases you may never actually know for sure what was done or accomplished.

This isn't to say that fuzziness has no virtues. Here is one author's attempt to make what he calls a crystal-clear statement on the virtues of vagueness (the term he uses instead of fuzziness):

> . . . vagueness in goal formation has many positive virtues. It leaves room for others to fill in the details and even modify the general pattern; over-precise goals stifle initiative. Vagueness may make it easier to adapt to changing conditions; ultra-precision can destroy flexibility. Vagueness may make it possible to work towards many goals that can only be attained by indirection. . . . Above all, vagueness is an essential part of all agreements resulting from compromise. When a dispute is resolved, some degree of ambiguity enters into the terms of settlement. Hence the wide-open language often used in the final language of statutory law. Similar ambiguities are found in most constitutions, charters, declarations of purpose, policy [statements], manifestos, and collective bargaining agreements. Certain anticipated situations are always referred to in terms that mean different things to different people, and are valuable because of, not despite, this characteristic.[4]

[4] Bertram Gross, *The Managing of Organizations* (New York: Free Press, 1964).

How Delegation Makes Us Feel Deficient

By not facing up to the basically fuzzy, vague character of objectives, the standard approach to delegation can create unrealistic expectations and harmful attitudes. The boss tends to feel uncomfortable admitting he is not really clear about exactly what is wanted. So he may try to *sound* clear and precise, even to the extent of making spurious statements about the situation. What is worse, after these apparently logical statements have been repeated long enough, the boss actually begins to believe in them himself. As a consequence, he resents spending more time later on to further define the objective, because a clear objective should not need continual explanation or modification.

The subordinate also tends to believe that the boss knows what he wants, because this makes life seem more structured and secure. The subordinate likes the notion of a clear objective that leaves him full freedom in carrying out the objective. But as he gets deeper and deeper into an assignment, he finds things are more and more complicated. He finds new information, additional options, unexpected problems. All of a sudden he has too many choices to make and too few guidelines. Yet the subordinate feels that continual checking back with the boss is a sacrifice of his all-important autonomy. Besides, he feels that if he does so he will either be admitting his own inadequacy or implying that the boss has been fuzzy and vague.

If an objective is not clear, then it would seem that either the boss or the subordinate (or both) must be deemed in some way deficient.

MANAGEMENT *of* OBJECTIVES

The very term "objective" acts to reinforce the set of false expectations and feelings of inadequacy. "Objective" implies something independent of the mind—something "real" or "actual," the very opposite of "subjective." We talk as if we are managed and controlled *by* these concrete things called objectives. Nonsense! We do not serve objectives, it is they that serve us. It is we who are in charge; it is management that creates and controls objectives, not the other way around. When progress toward an objective is checked along the way, unfavorable results are just as likely to indicate *a need to modify the objective* as to alter the type of actions being taken. We ought to talk about management *of* objectives, not management *by* objectives.

The Initial Defuzzing

Although some fuzz is inevitable and even helpful, I would certainly admit there is merit in attempting to clarify objectives— to make them as specific, complete, and measurable as possible. There is no point in living with more fuzz than you have to.

For instance, if you realize that any objective states only part of a whole bundle of constraints, then some discussion of the rest of the bundle would be very appropriate. In other words, after an objective is carefully stated, the boss and subordinate might go on to discuss, say, at least ten additional constraints or conditions that seem pertinent. Not only will such a list be useful in itself, but it will serve as a reminder to both boss and subordinate that there's a lot more involved in the objective than what is formally stated.

In making such a list, however, the tendency will be to dwell primarily on negative conditions and constraints rather than areas of freedom or independence. Eric Berne, the psychologist who developed transactional analysis, points out that: "Negatives are usually said loud and clear, with vigorous enforcement, while positives often fall like raindrops on the stream of life, making little sound and only small ripples." [5]

By negatives, Berne means prohibitions or constraints. By positives, he means permissions or liberties—that is, the person's freedom to follow out his own inclinations. *In exploring the meaning of an objective, permissions as well as prohibitions should be clarified.* For example, take the objective of finding a new sales manager for the new Midwestern branch by the end of next month. Assume that the salary, experience, and so forth,

[5] Eric Berne, *What Do You Say After You Say Hello?* (New York: Grove Press, 1972).

are also already specified in the objective. Further discussion might develop such conditions as these:

1. Subordinate can make the final choice (permission), but boss will interview candidate before he is officially signed on board (prohibition).
2. Subordinate can feel free to discuss assignment with the marketing or advertising people (permission), but not with the personnel department (prohibition).
3. Boss has no objections to recruiting from competitors (permission), with the exception of the Fitzgit Company (prohibition).
4. Boss realizes subordinate may miss the deadline on one or two of his other projects because finding the new sales manager is top priority (permission).
5. Subordinate must coordinate his hiring dates with the real estate department, which is lining up the appropriate facilities (prohibition).

Notice that this further exploration of the objective includes what might normally be considered "means" as well as "ends," which is perfectly appropriate once you accept the impossibility of cleanly separating them. Developing a list of additional conditions need not be a lengthy project. It is surprising how much can be cleared up in a short time by pushing for no more than ten or so additional prohibitions or permissions.

Follow Up on Fuzz

Developing a list of further conditions to an objective should help convince a boss and subordinate that much about the objective still remains fuzzy. But even if everything seems perfectly clear, they should not presume this idyllic situation will last for long. *The likelihood of further fuzz should be explicitly recognized and even planned for.*

The standard approach to delegation does talk about the need for periodic checking, but the primary purpose of such follow-up is primarily to assess *progress*. What I am suggesting is that an integral part of any follow-up sessions should be explicit attention to *further clarification*. Neither the boss nor the subordinate can possibly think of or cover all the necessary details at the start.

I am not proposing that several weeks later the subordinate stagger in to the boss saying something like, "Boy, this thing is really confusing. I'm just not sure which way to turn." Nor do I mean for the subordinate to return to the boss with just a set of general questions or problems, although this is what frequently occurs. Such actions by the subordinate place too much of the burden back on the boss's shoulders. The boss may rightfully resent or resist this, with the ultimate result that the delegation process really does break down.

Follow-up sessions are most effective when the subordinate has done his homework and comes in with a *specific list* of additional prohibitions or permissions that he wants his boss to confirm or deny. I would also urge that the subordinate report back on what he is *not* doing as well as what he is doing. For example, in trying to find a new sales manager for the Midwestern branch, the subordinate might point out that he has decided *not* to recruit at any competing companies because the sales people told him they thought this would hurt their own image in the marketplace.

Beyond the Impossible Dream

The impossible dream of riskless freedom continues to sound forth its siren call while in the real world of management the battles between freedom and security rage on—with security generally gaining the upper hand. The boss tends to covertly sneak glances over his subordinate's shoulder while both he and the subordinate resent the apparent need for such checking up. The subordinate tends to quietly shy away from making any decisions he doesn't have to make, while both he and the boss grow angry at this failure to exercise initiative.

Strange to say, it is the standard approach to delegation that contributes greatly to the domination of the security factor. While delegation ostensibly focuses on providing freedom, it assumes the existence of clear lines of authority, precise measures of performance, and specific objectives. When these conditions do not exist (which is most of the time), the freedom involved in delegation is quickly subverted by the aroused concern for security.

MBO stresses that subordinate freedom lies in taking action to achieve the objectives. Bosses are forever saying, "Get it done. I don't care how you do it, just get it done." But of course the boss does care how it gets done. When the subordinate inadvertently upsets the applecart, the boss storms in accusing him of poor judgment and demanding to know why this wasn't checked out with him first.

To get beyond the impossible dream, we must go beyond the standard approaches—which are based on unrealistic premises that lead both boss and subordinate to experience feelings of inadequacy and frustration. Why not acknowledge at the outset that *carrying out an objective is a kind of groping process; that many aspects of the objective may not have been initially clarified or discussed; that any action taken to achieve an objective is likely to affect the objective itself?*

Starting from these premises should allow the boss to feel much less defensive when he is unable to definitively state the objective at the start. Modifying the objective should then seem quite the order of the day as the subordinate goes to work and learns more about the situation. The subordinate may come to realize that *much of his initiative and freedom resides in the responsibility for further defining and clarifying objectives.* And it is precisely this kind of clarification which can reduce the inevitable risk of taking important actions to achieve an objective.

If delegation and MBO represent kinds of groping, then often the lion's share of the groping falls to the subordinate. Perhaps it is *this responsibility for groping that is in reality what is being delegated;* and shaping the ends as well as the means is a continuing process, not a one-shot matter as is so often assumed.

In the end, of course, achieving objectives must remain to some degree a joint responsibility of *both* boss and subordinate. Discretion is not something a boss gives a subordinate. Discretion is something that both boss and subordinate must exercise in the groping process of managing objectives—the process of defining and clarifying objectives even as they are being carried out.

4:
REORGANIZE –
When You Don't Know
What Else to Do

There'll Be Some Changes Made Today

What kind of beast is reorganization and where does it fit in the management kingdom?

At this very moment in countless conference rooms across the country, groups of managers are quietly assembling. For several weeks now the rumors have been flying fast and furious; managers have exchanged nervous jokes as they try to pick up the latest scuttlebutt. At long last the study group has completed its careful analysis; the various powers in the organization have all formally pleaded their case and informally politicked as much as seemed judicious. Now, in each meeting room, a hush falls over the fearful crowd as a senior executive rises, cracks the usual introductory joke, and then launches into the long-awaited announcement of a major corporate reorganization.

The announcement may involve the establishment of a group vice president plus the consolidation of several staff departments; a switch from functional management to product management; or perhaps a change from product management to a team approach. The reorganization might involve decentralizing foreign operations, regrouping the sales effort around clusters of customer industries rather than customer geographical locations, or perhaps creating a new department to deal with environmental affairs or equal opportunity employment.

At this same moment, every major management consulting firm is in the midst of several studies which will ultimately result in future reorganization announcements just like those mentioned above. Exact figures on the number of reorganizations are difficult to come by. Partners of several major consulting firms have estimated that most large industrial corporations reorganize in some major way at least once every two or three years.

Reorganizations are not exclusive to private business. Hospitals, universities, and many other nonprofit institutions are increasingly involved in periodic reorganizations. Even the supposedly stodgy federal government participates in rather frequent reorganizations. The past decade alone has witnessed the consolidation of scattered functions into two new departments (Transportation plus Housing and Urban Development); the establishment of several new agencies, such as the Office of Economic Opportunity (which has already been disbanded) and the Environmental Protection Agency; and numerous reorganizations within agencies such as the U.S. Postal Service and the Office of Management and Budget.

There is a vast management literature debating the best way to structure organizations, or questioning whether there is one best way. Organizational structure has been viewed in terms of a machine-like bureaucratic model; as a more natural, biological model which takes account of human variables; as an open system interacting with its environment. Theoreticians have recommended organizing around technology, information flows, decision-making processes, managerial functions, products, customers, geography, and many other bases.

It is not my intent to add further to this awesome panorama of hypotheses about the best structure for an organization. This chapter is more about the fundamental nature of reorganization— any reorganization. *What is special about reorganizing, and for what situations is it most appropriate?* My basic observation is that the true character of reorganization is widely misunderstood, and this misunderstanding itself contributes to the disappointment that surrounds so many reorganizations. I also believe that by clarifying our understanding of the fundamental nature of reorganization, we can develop better ways to increase the odds of success.

What Can You Change?

Reorganization is rarely an end in itself; rather, it is one of many approaches for working on organizational problems—one of many ways to make a change. The ultimate goal of most change is to modify the outputs or results of the activities performed by the organization. Traditionally the outputs of an organization were viewed only as profit, production of goods, or delivery of services—in other words, those objectives directly related to the economic mission of the organization. More recently, the view of outputs has been extended to encompass the personal satisfactions experienced by the organization's employees. Thus, nowadays changes may be made to affect personal as well as economic outputs of an organization.

One way to change the outputs of an organization is by modifying what people are doing (i.e., their tasks or activities). Another tactic for changing outputs is to alter the way people *perform* their tasks or activities (i.e., change the methods, procedures, or technology). Changing tasks or procedures would be relatively straightforward if it weren't for the fact that people are involved. Even fully automated situations end up involving people at some point or other.[1]

Thus, most changes in organizations ultimately involve modifying the behavior, skills, or attitudes of people. In order to see where reorganization fits into the scheme of things I find it useful to start by dividing the approaches for changing people into three categories (which, as usual, are somewhat interrelated):

1. Shift *bodies;* i.e., bring in a different person who already represents the desired change in attitudes, skills, or behavior.
2. Keep the body but shift the *mind* through some form of communication; i.e., try to get the same person to act differently by explaining what changes are desired and then ordering, persuading, or training the person to adopt those changes.
3. Alter the *environment* around the person in ways that will induce the desired changes in attitudes, skills, or behavior. Key environmental factors would include the following:
   a. incentive and control systems;
   b. allocation of resources such as money, manpower, equipment, and information;

---

[1] In any case, modifying a fully automated production line is not exactly a breeze. Diagnosing exactly what changes are needed can be tricky; changes made on one part of the line don't always work the first time and may have unanticipated effects on other parts of the line; and there is always considerable debugging time needed.

c. organization structure—which is what I am calling reorganization.

The CIA Character of Reorganization

Changing the structure of an organization is not a simple action that deals with just a few elements of organizational life. Reorganization uproots whole chunks of organization life and transplants them. For the people involved, it is much like moving to a new home in another part of a big city. Worn-out furniture may be junked in the process of moving or it may be discarded because it does not fit in with the new surroundings. Stores in the new area must be checked out to determine the prices and quality of the goods or services. New friendships may flourish just as old ones founder. Daily routines of travel, housekeeping, or recreation all undergo some modification.

Reorganization usually affects a far wider range of things than the other environmental types of change. In fact, a change in structure almost always ends up affecting other elements of the environment, such as incentives and allocation of resources, although such changes may not be by design. In addition, reorganization typically involves substantial changes in tasks and methods or procedures, including patterns of decision-making or problem-solving (again, not always by conscious intent).

Explicitly, reorganization is focused on changing relationships among people or groups of people, and such relationships tend to be complex, difficult to control, and hard to measure. The difficulties of reorganization are even greater because reorganization is a kind of indirect strategy. The idea is to *induce* changes in tasks, methods, or people by creating the appropriate structural conditions. A reorganization cannot specify all the intimate details of how the new structure will function; there is simply too much uncertainty and too many variables to permit rigorous predictions or highly specific objectives. Failure to understand these characteristics of reorganization often generates more than one kind of confusion.

For summary purposes I like to talk about the CIA nature

of reorganization (an acronym not without some relevant overtones):

Complex—involves whole chunks of organizational life; i.e., deals with many variables at once.

Intangible—emphasizes human interactions and group relationships which are difficult to quantify or control.

Abstract—a relatively high-level strategy that does not attempt to deal explicitly with the nitty-gritty.

Resorting to Reorganization

The seriousness of a situation is often regarded as the main justification for reorganizing—for instance, significant overcapacity (or undercapacity), a sharp drop in revenues or profits, potentially more rigorous enforcement of government legislation, high employee turnover. Yet many serious situations do not necessarily produce a reorganization. What else, then, must characterize a situation to make reorganization likely?

The management literature is rather silent on this question. Statements by executives about reorganization tend to be long-winded, rambling, and vague. For instance, in 1975 Mazda Motors of America Inc. disclosed a "major reorganization" that among other things was to transfer distribution rights and responsibilities in 18 Eastern states to C. Itoh and Company, a big Japanese trading firm. Mazda officials explained the purpose of the reorganization like this:

> The reorganization will provide increased financial resources, better administrative controls and greater responsiveness to the particular needs of the 385 Mazda dealers currently located throughout the U.S. The link with Itoh is intended to provide increased availability of funds and to strengthen management depth.[2]

Other typical justifications for reorganization include statements like these:

[2] "Toyo Kogyo's Mazda Subsidiary Discloses 'Major Reorganization,' " *The Wall Street Journal,* January 14, 1975.

We have a problem getting our plants together on things and we need a more consistent company policy.

We need a way to coordinate diverse projects and make sure everyone involved is taking the broad view of what will benefit the organization most.

The idea is to achieve better implementation of our overall programs as well as to create consistency with our newly acquired operations.

We need to reduce the destructive conflict between certain groups and facilitate better communication between them.

For managers who pride themselves on being analytical and precise, such statements seem unusually devoid of clear definitions of problem symptoms or causes. Yet think of a highly specific, well-defined problem: for example, making sure purchasing notifies production about delays in the shipment of raw materials; increasing the amount of time salesmen spend on the road; holding all managers responsible for employing a certain percentage of women in their groups. While these problems might be serious, none of them seem to require a reorganization. In fact, I find it hard to think of any specific type of problem that compels reorganization, a puzzling situation to say the least.

After considerable frustration and a good deal of muddling, the answer finally hit me—and then, as usual, seemed perfectly obvious. No specific type of problem seems associated with reorganization. That is precisely the point. *It is primarily when a situation is fuzzy that reorganization may be appropriate.* When a problem is ill-defined, when the criteria for deciding are muddy, when there is no real consensus on goals, the situation can still be serious enough to require action. You might be able to clarify the situation given enough time and analysis, but you may not have that much time. And besides, many real situations are so complicated or murky that you may never completely understand them. Reorganization does permit you to move in the face of all this fuzziness.

Reorganizing when you don't know what else to do actually makes a lot of sense when you think of it. After all, reorganization is a broad-brush approach. Don't the CIA characteristics of reorganization make it an extremely appropriate strategy for situations which possess those same characteristics? Robert Townsend, the former president of Avis, has commented that "reorganizing should be undergone about as often as major surgery." [3] I think the analogy with surgery certainly captures the serious nature of reorganization, but in other respects it is highly misleading. Most surgery is not undertaken without a great deal of careful analysis to determine exactly what the problem is and precisely what is to be done once the patient is on the operating table. If I were forced to make a medical analogy, I would liken reorganization more to one of those powerful, general-spectrum drugs. But personally I prefer a comparison to hunting with rifle shot versus buckshot. If you know where the bull's-eye is, you're better off with a single bullet that can really make some direct impact. If you don't know precisely where the target is, much less the bull's-eye, your odds of at least hitting the target are a lot better with buckshot.

Reorganization Is Two-Faced

In the opening paragraphs of this chapter, an anxious assembly of managers was awaiting the announcement of an impending reorganization. Can you imagine the senior executive's address sounding like the following?

> Gentlemen, as you know we face some very serious problems here at the Cryseas Corporation. Now we have spent a good deal of time studying the situation very carefully and we just cannot get a good fix on what the exact problem is. Oh, we do have some rough ideas of what's wrong, but the problems are complicated and involve many interconnected factors which we only dimly understand. We haven't been able to find any one or two simple steps to deal with the situation.
>
> As a result, we have decided to reorganize some of our activities in the hopes that this will give us a shove in the right direction. As you all know, reorganization is a chancy thing. It's hard to

[3] Robert Townsend, *Up the Organization* (New York: Knopf, 1970).

determine exactly how all the details will work out, but frankly, we don't know of a better approach to take at this time.

So I want you all to really get behind this reorganization effort and make it work! Here are the details. . . .

Managers have a well-trained reticence to admit that anything is muddy or poorly understood. It is considered even more reprehensible for a manager to recommend an imprecise, unfocused course of action, whatever the situation may be. Thus an executive who made a speech like the one above would no doubt be adjudged incompetent and the strategy of reorganization deemed a shoddy one—which, of course, is why no one talks about reorganization this way.

Instead, a seemingly more rational face gets painted onto a reorganization. The reorganization is tied in to specific goals like cutting costs or increasing productivity. Detailed analyses are made, attaching numbers to these objectives. The specific steps or actions involved in the reorganization are laid out with great care. A new arrangement of boxes on an organization chart accompanied by revised job descriptions makes the whole affair seem very concrete; and what could be more specific and tangible a step than physically moving offices around? In fact, the actions taken in a reorganization often are conceptually simple, tangible, and specific. It is the ramifications of the actions that are complex, intangible, and abstract.

So managers come to see *only* the rational face of reorganization. Even those who disagree with the reorganization find themselves compelled to couch their arguments in logical, analytical terms as they try to paint a less attractive, but nonetheless rational, face on the reorganization.

How Reorganization Fails

If there are few data on the number of reorganizations, there are even fewer formal reports on the success or failure of reorganizations. The lack of information is in part caused by the difficulty in setting up any rigorous criteria for determining the effectiveness of a particular reorganization. Moreover, motivation to judge success may also be lacking, because to some degree a reorganization is irreversible. Once a change in structure has begun to take hold, you cannot simply decide to revert back to the old structure and expect things to function the same way they used to.

Nonetheless, I would say that a good deal of disappointment is expressed about many reorganizations, often in terms like these:

> I'm not so sure but what this whole reorganization thing was a power play on the part of Dave and his boys. Of course we've got some serious problems, but I don't see how the reorganization is doing very much about them. I just don't think the boys upstairs really dug out the key issues. In any case, I can think of a lot simpler things to do.

> Look, this reorganization was supposed to make it easier to coordinate with the other departments and get things through channels faster. Now it just takes me twice as long to get things done; and where is all that money we were supposed to save?

> It seems to me that our management committee just didn't think through the details on this one. Oh, I suppose things are working a little more smoothly in some ways, but this damn reorganization has created a whole carload of new problems. Overall, I'm not sure but what we're worse off than before.

It's possible to see in these statements no more than the normal attachment to the status quo—that is, the usual, expected resistance to any change. Upon a closer look, however, I think you will find that each of the statements hints at a different, but common, source of trouble in reorganizations:

1. The use of reorganization to make something clear into something fuzzy
2. The creation of unrealistic expectations which the reorganization cannot live up to
3. The assumption that reorganization can group common activities together
4. The failure to provide any mechanism for effectively cop-

ing with the detailed problems inevitably created by a reorganization

One by one, let me amplify each of these four types of problems.

NOT ALL THAT FUZZY

The broad-brush character of reorganization .is sometimes
purposely used to camouflage or cover up a relatively clear-cut
objective—an objective that might not prove acceptable if it were
dealt with directly and explicitly. In other words, the situation is
not all that fuzzy; the proponents of the reorganization know
quite specifically what they hope to accomplish as well as understanding that the CIA character of reorganization will cloud their
intent. The precise objective might be the "power grab" referred
to in the first quotation above; it might be an attempt to cover
up an earlier mistake; it might be the diversion of unpleasant or
difficult tasks onto the shoulders of some other group; it might
be an effort to bolster the shaky status of a department or even
to reward some specific individuals. If the real agenda of such
reorganizations becomes apparent, then a good deal of resent-
ment can be unleashed, especially because the objective was
accomplished in an indirect or seemingly underhanded fashion.

Of course, reorganization may also be unwittingly applied to
a situation that seems fuzzy but is really not.

The Eyeglass Division of a large company had developed a line of
eye-measurement equipment (EME) which was losing money.
Corporate top management conducted a cursory review of the
situation and decided to move the EME line into the Optics Division,
which was one of many high-technology groups located at corporate
headquarters. The executives admitted they weren't too clear about
the exact nature of the EME troubles. They felt the problems had a
good deal to do with the highly technical nature of the product line.
They observed that most of the management at the Eyeglass Division
were not very sympathetic to the EME line and were probably not
knowledgeable enough to fully understand the complex technology
on which the EME products were based.

After the reorganization, the EME line fared no better, and a corporate
troubleshooter was finally called in to analyze the situation. He

uncovered the basic problem rather quickly. There was simply a very limited market for the EME line as it was currently constituted. Reorganization was not the answer. Money to re-engineer the products for a broader market was. Or else, of course, the firm could attempt to sell off the EME line to some other company that had a broader, related product line and could therefore market the EME products at a very low incremental cost.

In still other situations, management may fully understand the specific nature of the problems it would like to solve but may fail to fully grasp the CIA characteristics of the reorganization strategy. For instance, setting up a new department can seem like a simple, focused step to deal with a set of special problems, but may end up only creating confusion as people are switched around, lines of authority are altered, and relationships shift to deal with the new group.

ERRONEOUS EXPECTATIONS

An earlier section of this chapter pointed out that most executives feel compelled to discuss or justify a reorganization in terms of specific, tangible benefits despite the fuzziness of a problem and despite the unfocused nature of the reorganization strategy. This rational face of reorganization sets up expectations about such things as reductions in overhead, greater speed in processing paperwork, and increased autonomy or cooperation. As the reorganization unfolds, however, these specific results may not materialize simply because it turns out they were not what the reorganization was truly about.

For example, consider the case of two hospitals in a major metropolitan area that wanted to merge:

The two hospitals specialized in the same areas of medical care. The merger was discussed in terms of eliminating duplication of services and reducing staff. Also, both boards of directors felt that the combined entity would be able to mount more successful fund-raising appeals to the community.

The merger was consummated, but even after several years of integration no staff had been eliminated and costs had not been reduced at all. During informal discussions about these problems with a management consultant, several directors finally said, "Look, I think we were just kidding ourselves about all that cost-cutting business. What we were really concerned about was giving better service and better medical care. It's very important that we have high-quality, modern equipment. On these counts overall, the merger has really been very successful, although we certainly have had some problems."

The consultant went on to ask why the goal of better medical care had not been presented as the reason for merging in the first place. The gist of the directors' answer was that at that time the issues weren't as clear as they had now become in hindsight. Moreover, the goal of better health care is rather vague. How do you measure the quality of care? Does increasing quality mean higher costs, and might this not make the care less accessible to some people? Who would decide what better care means?

The point is that the situation was fuzzy and the reorganization strategy was quite appropriate. In fact, the reorganization was rather successful, but there was still considerable disappointment because of the erroneous expectations generated by the initial justification of the merger.

The most likely outcomes of any reorganization are that it will not achieve the exact goals stated at the start and that it is certain to create new problems, many of which will have been unforeseen.

YOU CAN'T WIN THE COMMONALITY GAME

In 1937 Luther Gulick, a member of President Roosevelt's Committee on Administrative Management, wrote his classic memorandum on the theory of organization. One of the most important organizational concepts stressed in this document was the "principle of homogeneity"—that is, work units in an organization should be structured so as to bring together people involved in similar kinds of activities.[4] In 1949 the First Hoover Commission further emphasized the importance of grouping agencies by major purposes, so that "by placing related functions cheek-by-

[4] Luther Gulick, "Notes on the Theory of Organization," in *Papers on the Science of Administration,* edited by Luther Gulick and L. Urwick (New York: Institute of Public Administration, 1937).

jowl the overlaps can be eliminated, and of even greater importance coordinated policies can be developed." [5]

Gulick's principle of homogeneity, or the cheek-by-jowl approach, still serves as the ostensible backbone of many a reorganization today. The categories of homogeneity (or "commonality," the term I prefer to use) outlined by Gulick in 1937 still have widespread currency: [6]

1. By major purpose (or goal) being served; e.g., organizing around separate product or service lines
2. By the process being used; e.g., management functions such as production, accounting, sales
3. By the persons or things dealt with or served; e.g., type of customer
4. By the place where activity is performed; i.e., by location or geography

A number of additions or refinements to these bases of commonality have developed over the years, such as the following:

1. Grouping on the basis of common knowledge, abilities, and skills required by the work
   (a) Cognitive modes; e.g., creative, analytical
   (b) Managerial duties; e.g., supervision, controlling, mediating, planning
   (c) Professional background; e.g., science, sociology, economics
2. Grouping to avoid conflict of interest
   (a) Separating performance of an activity from watchdogging or evaluation of that activity; e.g., separating quality control from production, or auditing from bookkeeping
   (b) Separating implementation of an idea from its development
3. Grouping around various decision-making or problem-

[5] Commission on Organization of the Executive Branch of the Government, *General Management of the Executive Branch*. A Report to the Congress, February 1949.
[6] Gulick, op. cit.

solving systems and processes; e.g., control processes, information systems, planning cycles

Theoretically, the principle of commonality certainly does help eliminate overlap, duplication, and confused or broken lines of authority or responsibility. What is often not realized is that, in practice, you can never really win the game of commonality. You neatly tuck all the loose ends under the various tents only to find that some other things are now sticking out somewhere else. You regroup to increase geographical commonality only to find you have now clustered together dissimilar products (or vice versa). You organize around major product lines only to find you have now mixed together too many different kinds of management functions or duties.

The commonality game is made even more difficult because within each of the categories listed above there may be many alternative (and incompatible) bases of commonality. For instance, suppose you want to organize around serving customers. You still face a choice of classifying customers by size of purchase (actual or potential), by type of industry, or by the use to which customers put the product sold them. The game is also complicated by the fact that a specific activity often does not cleanly fit into a particular category. For instance, is a service department part of the sales function, or the marketing function, or is it an extension of the production function?

Each year the commonality game grows more complex, for several reasons. First, most organizations are growing larger (or at least want to). Size brings new products, new customers, new skills, and so on, all of which disturbs the existing commonality. Second, the general advancement of factual knowledge and technology tends to increase the diversity of activities within an organization; for instance, automation and computers increase (not decrease) the variety of activities. Third, awareness of new connections and interrelationships among activities is constantly growing, which creates additional bases for commonality. Thus in recent years environmental quality, community relations, safety, equal opportunity employment, and consumer protection have all made their way into the commonality game.

But the inventive spirit of management has not been idle. New forms of organization are evolving that attempt to cope with the growing complexities of the commonality game. There is the project-management or task-force form of organization. Dual reporting systems and the "matrix" form of organization attempt to deal simultaneously with two different dimensions of commonality—for example, functional task *and* goal or purpose. Other attempts have been made to organize around different types of commonality at different levels of the organization; a division may be product-based while at lower levels the organization is skill-based or customer-based.

Alas, even organizing simultaneously along three dimensions would still not enable you to win the game of commonality. In simple physical terms, there is no way to lay out a building so that every group is next door to or across the hall from all the groups with which it has something important in common.

Still, there's nothing wrong with playing the game of commonality in reorganizing, so long as you realize what kind of game you're playing. Certainly at a specific time in the life of a given organization, one type of commonality may become more important than it was. Regrouping to enhance this new type of commonality may be very appropriate. All too often, however, we forget that *the best we can do is to exchange one kind of commonality for another*. People are surprised and upset because after a reorganization certain things are harder to coordinate than before.

Commonality also can mislead people regarding the basically fuzzy and groping nature of reorganization. The doctrine of commonality has been so well accepted for such a long time that it seems like something relatively simple, concrete, and specific. Analyzing a fuzzy situation in terms of commonality appears to reduce much of the fuzz. Thus, regrouping to remedy certain lacks of commonality makes reorganization appear a very logical, precise strategy. But regrouping on some basis of commonality does very little to mitigate the CIA character of reorganizing. Big chunks of life are still being moved around, group relationships are being changed, and commonality says very little about dealing with the daily nitty-gritty.

SORTING OUT THE DETAILS

Reorganization of necessity ruptures many of the carefully spun strands that make up the intricate web of organizational life. Even strands that were thought to lie well outside the boundaries of the reorganization may be bruised. Almost no reorganization attempts to deal with every part of the organization, yet often there are subtle ties between those parts which are reorganized and those which are not. The apparent boundaries of any reorganization are rather artificial; the web of relationships is irregular and multidimensional, and can rarely be neatly segmented into totally independent networks.

What do reorganization plans generally prescribe for binding up or re-forming the delicate, complex web that is so necessary for an organization to function effectively? Usually not very much. Reorganization is by its nature a kind of abstract philosophy of change that offers only a few rather general guidelines for handling the myriad details that must somehow be worked out. Changed (new) relationships among people require "debugging" even more than do new machines, and many of the bugs just cannot be accurately anticipated or predicted, even with very thorough analysis. *The reorganization itself usually provides no mechanism for effectively coping with all the detailed problems it creates,* and certainly provides no guarantee that all the details will be properly sorted out.

The French have a nice verb to describe this disentangling, sorting-out process: *debrouiller.* It is curious that there is no good translation in English for this verb. The following anecdote explains more clearly its exact meaning:

During World War II a Frency army squadron was marooned in the African desert. Supplies were very low, and the soldiers' clothing were in tatters. Somehow a special shipment of Red Cross clothing got through to the remote base. The supply sergeant lined up all the men and proceeded to hand out the clothing in a peculiar but nonetheless orderly fashion: one shirt, one pair of pants, and two shoes to each man, but without any regard to size.

After each soldier had one (or two) of everything he was supposed to have, the sergeant bellowed the command, "Debrouillez-vous," or sort it out for yourselves. (Evidently the group did get things pretty well straightened out, except for one poor chap who found himself with two left shoes—and could find no one else who had two right shoes.)

A reorganization may well be a good general move; it can provide a nice shove in the proper direction. But if too many specific details do not get sorted out, these details can outweigh the more general benefits of the reorganization; they can easily cause the nice shove in the proper direction to jump the tracks— which is why . . .

Reorganization Is Never Enough

If reorganization is a broad-brush action painted on a fuzzy canvas, we can hardly expect reorganization alone to produce a true work of art. The preceding chapter suggested that even apparently precise objectives set by a boss with his subordinate should be viewed only as the start of a groping process; it suggested that such objectives must be continually refined and shaped in the very process of carrying them out. From this perspective, then, reorganization represents a rather extreme kind of groping process involving large numbers of people, not just a boss and subordinate. Reorganization is a kind of "group grope," if you will.

Changing organization charts and shifting people or offices are just the beginning of movement in a new direction, not the final or culminating step of a change process. *Reorganization is an ongoing, trial-and-error, zeroing-in sort of process, not a one-shot, definitive approach to change.* Reorganization poses the puzzling question of how to get where you would like to be when you don't know exactly where you're going.

FLEXIBILITY DOESN'T ALWAYS FOLLOW FROM FUZZINESS

As a reorganization progresses, certain more specific goals and priorities evolve and emerge. However, these emerging goals and priorities may in turn suggest the need for important modifications in the general scope of the reorganization. If reorganization is an imprecise, approximate approach, then during the process of reorganizing we can expect to discover that the initial approximation was somewhat off base, and we may have to alter the original thrust of the reorganization. Thus the initial guidelines for any reorganization must be somewhat flexible.

This may not sound like much of a problem, since reorganization is vague and general to begin with. The needed flexibility, however, is not necessarily provided by the fuzziness of a reorganization. For instance, centralization of purchasing authority may be a very general and imprecise strategy. I may subsequently discover that the real problem is the inability of salesmen to make accurate volume forecasts, but I may nonetheless decide to keep the purchasing function at headquarters. Often, reorganization creates a sense of commitment to a course of action. Modifying that commitment can be viewed as a loss of face or even an outright error unless the need for flexibility and the likelihood of potential modifications are recognized and admitted at the start.

Building flexibility into a reorganization strategy in a sense means looking at reorganization as an experiment, but not an experiment in the traditional sense. C. West Churchman explains nicely what I am driving at:

> In the classical theory of experimental design it is essential that the scientist decide beforehand what question he wishes to pose, and that he carefully define his concepts about what he observes. He is required throughout a well-controlled experiment to keep his purpose constant, and he is required not to change the meanings of his concepts. In some real sense, however, these requirements are unnatural. In the more natural mode of inquiry we rarely make our purposes clear, and we rarely keep the meaning of our concepts the same throughout the process of inquiring. A more natural experiment for many people may be the "elusive experiment" in which the process of experiment makes clear the purposes of experiment and aids us in developing the meanings of the terms we use.[7]

[7] C. West Churchman, *A Challenge to Reason* (New York: McGraw-Hill, 1968).

Reorganization would thus be what Churchman calls an "elusive experiment."

REORGANIZATION PLUS

As the details get sorted out in the process of reorganization, the situation becomes less fuzzy. As the problems become clearer and more precise, other, more focused types of change can be introduced. Here is a case history that illustrates what I mean:

The Britebuoys Corporation was a large manufacturer of semi-custom mechanical components with an excellent reputation for quality. Britebuoys' share of market had been dropping for some time. After studying the problem, the top management committee concluded that they were losing business because their competitors were paying more attention to customer service.

A major reorganization was launched to improve customer service. A special group of service representatives was set up to assist the sales force. As part of the manufacturing operation, a project-management system was set up in each production plant. The project manager was assigned certain important (large dollar) orders and was supposed to act as an expediter for these orders. If the order ran into production troubles, the project manager was in charge of seeing that the problems were unsnarled and communicating with the customer if this were necessary. The project manager also became the point of contact within each plant for any salesman or service representative who wanted information about the status of the order or who wanted to relay some information from the customer.

The reorganization generated a good deal of conflict. Salesmen felt the service representatives were taking away their contact with the customer. The service representatives felt the project managers should clear things through them. A number of the production groups became very upset with the project managers. Finally the executive vice president appointed a small task force to try and figure out what was really causing all the turmoil.

One of the things the task force discovered was that what most customers actually wanted was faster delivery of their orders. As a result, the salesmen and service personnel were putting great pressure on the project managers for quick turnaround time. The project managers, in turn, were putting a lot of pressure on the quality people to loosen their standards. But *the quality-control group had no real stake in speeding up deliveries. Their whole incentive system depended on minimizing the number of products rejected by the customers.*

A similar situation was occurring with inventory. Pressure had been applied to increase general levels of stock in order to avoid long delays from out-of-stock positions. But one of the important controls at Britebuoys was return on investment (ROI). *An increase in inventory (and related warehousing costs) threatened to adversely affect the ROI targets* of the responsible groups.

The task force also discovered that the purchasing department was not doing all it could to expedite deliveries from suppliers. This task had never been of great importance in the past, so *most of the purchasing agents were not really sure what techniques were most appropriate for pushing their suppliers.* The task force recommended a quick bit of training in the techniques of "show and tell" (making suppliers clarify exactly where they were in processing an order), follow-up, and so forth.

Let me isolate the several types of additional change that were required in this little case history—types of change which are likely to be needed in a good many reorganizations.

First, *at the heart of most reorganizations there is likely to be a shift in priorities* (although the exact shift may not be clear at the outset). Of necessity, some goals and objectives drop in importance as others are pushed to the fore. In the case of Britebuoys, speedy delivery became more important as quality and ROI became less so. Merely changing certain structural elements through a reorganization is rarely enough to drive home a specific shift in priorities.

Second, *most shifts in priorities require some modification of existing controls and incentive systems.* Usually the existing incentives and controls have evolved over a long period of time and they strongly reinforce the existing priorities, not the new priorities that may emerge during a reorganization. Thus, at Britebuoys the quality-control incentive system and the ROI control both needed some modification. In other cases it may be the bases for promotion, the personnel system, or the budget allocation criteria that need modification.

Third, *a shift in priorities often requires the development of new skills or attitudes* on the part of some employees (e.g., the shipping department, among others, at Britebuoys). The structural shifts of a reorganization are seldom sufficient to create the new attitudes, although they may help. New skills do not magically appear simply because boxes have been shifted around on the chart. *Major educational and training programs are usually very important for the success of any major reorganization.* All too often, top management provides no more than a long memo plus a few orientation meetings and blames any problems that develop on a natural resistance to change, which they hope will wear off in time.

"LOOK AS YOU LEAP"

If reorganization is a groping process, it need not be a blind grope. It can rely on *selective* trial and error; it can become a form of *organized* muddling. But who is in charge of a reorganization? Someone makes the announcements, some person or group draws up the final plans, somebody may check to see that the physical changes are made—but usually none of these people or groups is in charge of overseeing the whole reorganization. And no single group involved in the reorganization is likely to have full control over it, or even to have the full picture of what's going on.

Sometimes the executive to whom all the reorganized groups report may feel responsible for seeing how things are going. Often, however, the person who fits this description is the president or some other very high-level official who has many other duties vying for his attention, and tracking all the details of a major reorganization can be a very complex and time-consuming chore.

Clearly, *there is a need for setting up some kind of group that can monitor the progress of the reorganization,* and the plans for such a monitoring activity should be part of the initial reorganization blueprint. The plans need not be fuzzy and vague, even though the reorganization itself is.

Yes, this monitoring requires manpower and therefore money,

but after all, reorganization is a serious matter. Yes, such monitoring is a difficult task, but it can be done—and has in some instances been done with notable success.

The monitoring group may serve several functions. It may act as a clearinghouse for the inevitable flood of unexpected problems that arise. The group members may also attempt to synthesize their observations and those of others in order to gain an increasingly clear overview of what is really happening. The monitoring group may make recommendations for modifying the original reorganization plans or may propose additional types of change needed to implement the reorganization. In short, the job of the monitoring group is to look *as* the organization leaps.

Reorganization Is Powerful

If reorganization is a broad-brush strategy, if reorganization alone is never enough, this does not mean that reorganization is a weak approach for creating change. The structure of our lives has a powerful effect on the way we live. The groups we belong to, the groups we work with, the groups we live next to, and the bosses we report to exert an enormous influence over our behavior. A reorganization plops us smack in the middle of a new setting where it is very difficult to continue functioning the same way we used to. Reorganization creates a sharp break with the past; it is not the gradual change of one small thing at a time. If anything, the foregoing parts of this chapter should suggest that reorganization is a very powerful strategy—often more powerful than we realize.

In this section I want to single out a few of reorganization's powerful elements—elements whose power is not always fully comprehended.

SYMBOLS STAND FOR SOMETHING

If I work closely with a manager and know first-hand whether or not he is important in the organization, then I may not pay much attention to the symbol of the carpet on his office floor. In general, however, it is difficult for us to have an intimate first-hand knowledge of more than a very small segment of an organization's activities and personnel. Written reports and second-hand gossip may of course help fill in part of our knowledge gap, but we also rely heavily on symbols to provide us with a quick reading of things we don't know about first- or even second-hand. Titles, job levels, office decor, group size, and budget allocations are in some way symbols we rely on as a substitute for more intimate knowledge.

Of course a symbol is not the same thing as what it stands for; I may have a corner office with a window and still not be very important or well-paid. Yet symbols in and of themselves can often affect the very things they are supposed to represent: For example, I may actually *become* more important because many people rely on symbols that proclaim my importance and act as if I were important. In other words, I would disagree with Shakespeare's famous line and requote it like this: "An organization by a different name may not smell the same."

Reorganization has great power to manipulate or alter organizational symbols. Often, many of the key changes in a reorganization are of highly symbolic nature, as in this example:

In 1970 President Nixon reorganized the old Bureau of the Budget. One of the primary goals of the reorganization was to create a shift of priorities in the Bureau so that more attention would be given to management problems of the executive branch. Although the Bureau's original charter included a mandate to monitor management in the executive branch, the great majority of the Bureau's attention seemed always to end up focused on budgetary affairs. A top executive of the old Bureau who dealt primarily with nonbudgetary activities commented that: "Whenever I go into the field to talk about management, I just don't seem to get through. The agency people insist on seeing 'budget' writ large upon my forehead, and immediately launch into their funding problems."

Part of the reorganization's attempt to deal with this problem included changing the Bureau's name to the Office of *Management* and Budget. In addition, the reorganization placed new high-level appointees to head up several new groups established on the management side of the Office, to symbolize the increased stature of the nonbudgetary functions.

There are many other kinds of symbols that can be used in reorganizing. Making a group report to a more senior executive than it did before is a clear indicator of increased importance. The symbol of establishing a new group is a particularly interesting one. A new group (even with a succinct title) represents something unknown, something to which it is hard to apply old emotional reactions that develop toward symbols that have been around a long time. Thus it can be useful to set up a new group rather than transferring certain activities from one existing group to another. The group losing an activity to some other existing group often feels such a transfer will have the symbolic value of lowering its own prestige. If the same activity plus other activities from other groups is transferred to some new group, the symbolic meaning may be more one of contributing to a new effort.

PERMISSION TO CHANGE

Perhaps the most important symbolic aspect of any reorganization lies in the very implications of the term itself. The mere mention of the word "reorganization" suggests significant change; often the word is actually used as a synonym for the whole concept of change. It symbolically communicates that change is desirable and is the expected order of the day.

Eric Berne has observed that people often need permission to change their behavior—behavior which has typically developed from many years of what he calls "negative programming" (i.e., don't do this and don't do that). Berne cites a compulsive gambler who said, "I don't need someone to tell me to stop gambling, I need someone to give me *permission* to stop, because somebody in my head says I can't." [8] Reorganization is one way of symbolically granting this kind of permission to try out new kinds of behavior.

Of course, granting permission to change does not guarantee that change will occur. Moreover, the permission to change can cause some anxiety precisely because choices are opened up to

[8] Eric Berne, *What Do You Say After You Say Hello?* (New York: Grove Press, 1972).

reexamination. The fuzzy implications of the changes proposed in a reorganization may only add to the general tension of contemplating change. Still, reorganization is a very powerful approach for unfreezing deeply entrenched habits or patterns of action and unlocking the tenacious grip of tradition.

Rx for Reorganization

1. Do your homework. Try to sort out the problems, symptoms, and causes in a fuzzy situation. If you find you can pin them down, reorganization may not be the most appropriate strategy.
2. As you design the reorganization, be aware of its symbolic aspects and capitalize on them.
3. Admit to yourself (and possibly to the rest of the organization) that all the homework in the world won't adequately clarify the reasons for a reorganization, nor will it permit accurate prediction of all the problems that will emerge during the reorganization.
4. Build flexibility into the reorganization plans, and indicate your expectation that many modifications may occur as problems become clearer during the course of the reorganization.
5. Set up some formal mechanism to monitor the progress of the reorganization, to pick up problems as they develop, to crystallize the true goals as they emerge, and to communicate these new perceptions back to the reorganizing groups.
6. Above all, remember that reorganizing is what you do when you don't know what else to do—and that can be perfectly appropriate.

5:
DEALING WITH EXPERTS:
The Art of Managing from Ignorance

Ever More Experts

Despite all the propaganda for population control, the experts keep proliferating like rabbits. Each new area of knowledge, each new bit of technology nurtures its own brand of expert. Older forms of expertise don't seem to die (or even fade away); they just split in two or more and thereby multiply.

Some of the newer types of expertise are relevant not only to the products and services produced by organizations, but also to the very functions of management itself. New management specialties have sprung up—operations research, systems analysis, organization development, instructional design, and environmental planning, to name a few. Existing management functions demand ever more refined expertise. For example, a corporate controller no longer looks for just a good "numbers man"; he needs specialists in credit, insurance, portfolio investment, acquisitions, foreign exchange, and many other areas.

As the kinds of expertise have increased, so has the necessity for relating all the various specialties. Not so long ago, a manager might spend most of his career peacefully struggling only with problems in his own area. Now, every week most managers must deal with a number of other departments and their affiliated experts. Nor are all the experts in-house. Reliance on outside experts has mushroomed tremendously. For instance, according to data from the Association of Consulting Management Engineers (ACME), billings of management consultants rose from some $426 million in 1954 to roughly $850 million in 1968 to over $2 billion in 1974 (and these figures do not include the consulting work done by public accounting firms). Similar growth has occurred in the use of outside lawyers, architects, university professors, scientists, and other consultants.

How do managers cope with all these experts? The answer, I'm afraid, is "not very well."

"Fear" Is a Four-Letter Word

Unfortunately, experts don't usually come packaged with brand names that assure us of their quality. Nor do the various academic degrees or state licenses always serve as a very effective guarantee of competence. Many specialties don't even have any kind of certification program. There are no convenient "consumer guides to experts" that provide thorough and knowledgeable testing of the exotic experts with whom we may be required to deal. So, right off the bat we have something important to fear: picking or using a poor expert.

But even if we're completely convinced that the expert is thoroughly knowledgeable (and in fact he is), our worries are not over. We must usually work with the expert to help him accomplish what we want, and then we must somehow evaluate his work and act (or not act) on the basis of his advice. In all these dealings with experts, we may fear showing our ignorance (even though we may be entitled to it). We may also be afraid to put ourselves somewhat at the expert's mercy. Moreover, an expert often uncovers more problems than he solves. He may force us to focus on issues that we were able to ignore before.

In a more general sense, dealing with experts forces us to manage from ignorance, and that flies in the face of everything we have come to cherish and hold sacred about management. Oh, we have grown somewhat accustomed to managing when we're uncertain about the future, but in the present we're supposed to know more or less what we're talking about. This knowledge is what our background and experience are supposed to have provided. If we find ourselves managing from ignorance, then the generally advised prescription is to get some learning (and quickly). Each new area of expertise gives rise to a welter of books and courses for us to absorb if we can.

There is no question that the best way to deal with an expert is to become something of an expert yourself. The real question is how many areas you can become a real or even a quasi-expert in. Certainly if an area of expertise is of great significance to your job and will continue to be so over an extended period of time, then you'd better learn a lot about that field (e.g., as a controller you'd better know something about accounting and budgeting). Of course, it's often difficult to know which new specialty will turn out to be truly important and for how long.

A more difficult problem is what to do about all the experts you must deal with on a one-shot or very infrequent basis. And what about all the areas of expertise that are needed quite frequently but are of less than major importance to the job? What about a sudden need for expertise without sufficient time to become even a quasi-expert? I guess the prevailing philosophy would say that if you can't learn a lot then you ought to learn at least a little. If you can't be a quasi-expert, you should at least be a pseudo-expert. We take a quickie course entitled "Accounting for Non-Accountants" or "Everything You Wanted to Know About Statistical Decision-Making Under Uncertainty, But Were Afraid to Ask." If these courses don't give us all the answers, the hope is that at least they'll give us some of the questions, and perhaps an ability to comprehend some of the answers provided by the expert. But frankly, it's rather difficult to become even a good pseudo-expert in a few days' time, and we may not even have the time available to attend a two- or three-day seminar in every subject that we consult an expert about. Moreover, such seminars often only increase our fear and trembling about the complexities of the field, leaving us even more bewildered about how to deal with the specialists.

No wonder we try to avoid dealing directly with experts whenever possible. We claim the expert is not really needed; we keep putting off the decision to bring in an expert. Or perhaps we perfunctorily hire an expert, isolate him in some corner, and trot him out to public view every once in a while just so people can't accuse us of lacking expertise.

The premise of this chapter is that more and more managers are finding they must operate outside their immediate fields of knowledge, yet doing so is an art or skill which they have not developed to any high degree. I contend *it is possible to develop the skill of managing from ignorance, but only if we first admit that such a skill is a legitimate part of a manager's repertory.* The techniques suggested in this chapter are far from definitive or complete, but at the very least they demonstrate the possibility of developing such skills.

For the purposes of this chapter I will use the word "expert" to signify someone who has significant knowledge of a field about which the manager is relatively ignorant. The basic context will be that of a manager dealing with an expert outside the organization. This particular context was chosen because it forces confrontation with many of the more difficult problems of managing from ignorance. From careful observation of how managers actually deal with experts, I have tried to cull out (and make explicit) some of the approaches which seem most effective. I will also comment on a few of the less effective approaches that are commonly used for want of something better.

A General Strategy for Dealing with Experts

Our reactions to other people (and their work) depend to some degree on three interrelated variables: our observations, the judgments we put on our observations, and what we want from the other person. It is not too risky, then, to assert that

1. Some observations are easier to make than others.
2. Some observations are easier to judge than others.
3. Some observations are more relevant to what we want than others.

For example, a person's height is relatively easy to observe. It's also not too difficult to judge whether a person's height makes him exceptionally tall. As for what I want, height might be very relevant if I were seeking a good basketball player and irrelevant if I were looking for a good sales manager. Right?

Unfortunately, this is not the best of all possible worlds. Often, what is easy to observe is hard for us to judge, or what is easy for us to judge may not be very relevant to what we want. So we constantly make tradeoffs between ease of observation, ease of judgment, and relevance. Even in dealing with non-experts, we rely more than we realize on what is easily observable but not necessarily relevant. For example, the psychologist G. R. Thornton had some subjects evaluate photographs of various individuals and also had them rate individuals who appeared in person (without speaking). Those individuals wearing glasses tended to be rated consistently higher on such traits as honesty, intelligence, industriousness, and dependability.

Other research studies on managers suggest that good looks and height do increase the odds of climbing the corporate ladder. I suspect this kind of inappropriate tradeoff is even more prevalent when it comes to experts. Oliver Wendell Holmes's little verse about doctors could just as well have been about experts in general:

> Talk of your science! After all is said
> There's nothing like a bare and shining head!
> Age lends the graces that are sure to please;
> Folks want their Doctors mouldy, like their cheese.

When we interview someone whose skills are similar to our own, we try to find out something about the person's background and experience. From his conversation we informally observe his ideas and judge his positions. We note his use of key terms (or jargon), his awareness of new developments in the field, and his areas of ignorance. Many of these observations are not direct indicators of competence, biases, ethics, and the other things we're really interested it. But because we know something about the field, we're able to make reasonable correlations between these indirect observations and what is really relevant.

But when it comes to experts, it's much more difficult to make appropriate correlations. We're less sure of what to look for and how to judge the relevancy of what we observe. To deal with an expert, *we must make new and more extreme compromises between what is most relevant and what we feel most competent to observe or judge.* All the suggestions in the rest of this chapter are essentially ideas about ways to make better tradeoffs, but they still represent compromises. In dealing with experts we may be fighting with one hand tied behind our back, but there is still a great deal we can do with only one hand, if we work at it.

So You Need an Expert

When you first realize you might need an expert, there's a tendency to put off doing anything about finding one for as long as possible. This means that when you finally do have to hire an

expert, you're under great time pressure and are likely to do a poor job of selecting one.

Several years ago I made a survey of 20 small, technology-based firms. In the survey I asked each firm some specific questions about a recent expert they had hired. Over 50 percent of the firms indicated that less than three weeks had elapsed between their decision to find an outside expert and their actual hiring of the expert.

If you're under great time pressure to select an expert, you're likely to grab at the first one who comes along. In the same survey mentioned above, more than two-thirds of the managers said they had seen only one expert before making their choice. Yet it takes time to find a good expert, just as it takes time to find a good employee in a field you know something about.

Of course, even with plenty of time the first problem is that you need some names. The most common gambit is to call up a few business friends who you think may have used a similar kind of expert in the past. If your business friend "has been there," he can even give you an appraisal of the expert he finally used.

The trouble with this approach is that your friend may not know any more about the field than you do. He may also not have been very astute in selecting his expert. For that matter, your friend's appraisal of the expert whom he did use may not be very accurate either. Very few studies of experts in business have ever been made, but there is a study on doctors which bears out the point. (After all, doctors are experts we must all use and judge.) The study was made in North Carolina some years ago and showed that there was very little correlation between the feelings of a patient about his doctor and the actual competence of the doctor as determined by a panel of other doctors.

Still, you may feel that at least your friend can tell you whether the expert did an outstanding job or really fouled things up. Even assuming your friend's assessment of the outcome is accurate, however, it may not be very relevant unless you know the details of the situation, what factors contributed to the outcome, and how the expert was used and by whom.

The point is that *the user of an expert is often the least qualified to judge that expert's skill.* The closer someone is to being a true expert, the better able he is to select and judge another expert in the same field. If you can't find a friend or someone in your organization who is something of an expert in the appropriate field, you might try consulting your local university. Universities are excellent but often-overlooked sources for procuring expert references. Simply locate a professor who teaches in the special field in which you're trying to locate an expert. The professor is quite likely to know a number of the experts in his field and may even provide you with other useful information about the area of expertise in which you require help.

Interviewing the Expert

Most managers wouldn't think of hiring a non-expert without a careful interview, but they look at interviewing an expert as an exercise in futility. Often the interview with the expert ends up being merely an empty ritual. You describe your situation and the expert snows you with all his qualifications and past triumphs. After all, how can you really find out if the expert knows what he's talking about when *you* don't really know what he's talking about?

The answer is, you probably can't directly assess the expert's professional knowledge. By and large, you have to rely on the testimony of other experts acquainted with the work of the person you're interviewing (which is why the sources you use for picking up names of experts are so important). There are several things, however, which you can and should check out during the interview that will greatly increase your odds of selecting the right expert.

First, *see if the expert does a good job of trying to find out exactly what it is you want or need.* When you describe your problem or situation, does the expert assume he knows exactly what you're saying? Does he probe for more information? Does he assume he already knows most of the answers? The point is that on the job, the expert will probably have to help you crystallize and define what you want, and he'll have to use you (or your people) to help fill him in on the details of the situation.

If the expert doesn't manifest some ability to do this in the interview, the odds are he won't be much better at it on the job.

A second thing to look for is *how clearly the expert communicates*. While an expert must help you to give him the input he needs, he must also be able to translate back to you the results of his thinking. In particular, the expert should be both *able* and *willing* to explain to you what he is talking about. You might even make it a point to ask the expert to explain some technical or jargon phrase that has crept into his conversation. Even if you know a bit about the field, you're better off keeping such knowledge to yourself than trying to impress the expert with it.

Third, you should *assess the expert's experience,* but you can't do it in the same way you would in a field where you're more knowledgeable. Specifically, there are at least two important dimensions of his experience you can probe: the breadth of his experience and the relevance of his experience to your problems.

The breadth of the expert's experience can be a good indicator of his ability to grab onto the essentials of a new situation. Though your situation probably differs in some ways from what the expert has tackled before, it may not be as unique as you think. For instance, an architect who has built many different-sized plants for companies in a number of different industries is more likely to understand how to incorporate the special needs of your organization into his building design.

On the other hand, most fields of expertise have many subdivisions, and any one expert can hardly be fully experienced in more than a few of the subspecialties. It is particularly important to pin down the expert's subspecialties, because *most experts tend to claim more general expertise than they really have;* it's part of surviving in a competitive world. So, for example, if your new plant requires special sanitary or dust-free conditions, you should probably try to find an architect with some specific experience in such construction.

Of course, if you're really not an expert yourself it may be hard for you to know exactly how a given field of expertise breaks down into subspecialties. There is no reason, however, why you can't *ask the expert himself how he categorizes the various specialties in his field.* Then you can follow up by asking him for the rough percentages of his time spent in each of the areas he identifies. Many experts shy away from pinning themselves down like this, and in fact the expert may not know right off the top of his head exactly how his time or experience has been allocated. Sometimes you can help by asking him if he spends, say, 80 percent of his time in one area. He'll probably say no, but then you can keep trying other rough percentages until you zero in on an approximate allocation.

In assessing the breadth and relevance of the expert's experience you might keep these variables in mind.

—Industries in which the expert has worked.
—Departments or managerial areas in which the expert has worked. (Among other things, this can help you gauge whether the expert has worked closely with managers who lack the same expertise as you.)
—Size of previous projects handled. Is your project much larger than anything the expert has handled or much smaller? (The latter might make him regard it as insignificant or uninteresting.)

There is one other aspect of the expert's experience which many managers fail to explore: *What does the expert feel are his limitations;* in what areas does he feel less competent or less interested? There is nothing wrong in asking the expert flat out about this. Part of being an effective expert is knowing your limitations, and having enough sense to bring in help when you get in over your head.

As a general caveat I want to emphasize the importance of *probing the experience of the expert before you outline your own situation in much detail.* Of course this is a standard gambit in interviewing non-experts, in order to minimize the candidate's ability to slant his replies toward what he feels the interviewer would like to hear. Yet this time-tested approach is often ignored when interviewing an expert, perhaps because of our general fear of dealing with experts. As a matter of fact, it is doubly important not to expose your hand to the expert, just because you'll be much less able to detect the biases in his descriptions of his experience.

The fourth area you can usefully assess in an interview is *the expert's outside interests.* As George Bernard Shaw put it, "No man can be a pure specialist without being in the strict sense of the word an idiot." All of us play many roles in life: parent, spouse, struggling golfer, expert, subordinate, and so on. We're a bit different in each role, but there is a central core which remains much the same in all roles. Again, the gambit of asking about outside interests is standard for interviewing non-experts but is often overlooked in the expert interview. Since you can't directly assess the expert in his role of expert, it's all the more important that you catch some glimpse of the person in his other roles, which you can more easily evaluate. The way an expert approaches his outside interests can provide valuable clues about the way he deals with his professional specialty.

By now I hope you're convinced that there is plenty to talk about in an interview with an expert. It should also be clear that you need to interview the person(s) who will actually be doing the work for you. It can be a waste of time or highly misleading to talk only with the senior partner of a firm, or with a high-ranking officer who is good at landing accounts but has nothing to do with the actual work. Even if an outside firm has an excellent reputation as a whole, some of their experts are going to be a lot better than others. You can count on it.

One last suggestion is to *try and interview the expert in his own office.* You'll pick up a lot of extra information simply by seeing the surroundings in which the expert operates. You might even be fortunate enough to have your meeting interrupted by a phone call and have the chance to see your expert in action.

Managing Experts

Even if a manager interviews several experts and carefully makes his choice, he's still likely to plop his problems in the expert's lap, breathe a deep sigh of relief, and move on to other matters.

Managers often view an expert as a kind of "black box." Feed the box the necessary background and data, give the box a chance to operate, and come back later to collect the output. This is a most seductive concept, particularly because it fosters the dream of no supervision.

In reality, making effective use of an expert is rarely this simple, and *the way an expert is used contributes to the end result at least as much as the expert's professional knowledge or skill.* Lawyers, market researchers, computer experts, engineering specialists, management consultants, and most other experts all make the same major complaint: The great majority of clients do not use them very well.

You may argue, however, that it is the expert who should take major responsibility for seeing that he is effectively utilized. Who should know better how to use an expert than the expert himself? Unfortunately, the formal training of experts pays little attention to the problems of working with non-experts. Throughout the career of an expert, his major interest tends to be the development of his special knowledge or skill at problem-solving. Many experts seem to view dealing with clients as intrusions— necessary to the pursuit of their profession, but bothersome. To some degree a client can prod the expert into some thinking about how he can best be utilized, but in most cases the bulk of the responsibility for effective use of an expert falls to the client.

Managing an expert is not that much different from managing anyone else. Yet somehow the managerial techniques of supervision, setting objectives, and using budgets and other controls often seem to be disregarded. For instance, in the early sixties many firms increased their scientific-research activity. Scientists were thought to be a different breed of cat. They were given pleasant surroundings and basically left alone to pursue their exotic projects. When the results were disappointing, many firms learned that scientists, like everyone else, responded to deadlines and benefited from controls like budgets.

Experts are still people, and have most of the same human characteristics as everyone else. They are more interested in some projects than others. They have personal needs and goals which are not always compatible with the organizational tasks they are assigned. And all experts are not equally expert.

As you do with any other person who works for you or with you, it is important to become quickly aware of how your expert operates, to learn his biases and shortcomings so that you can compensate for them.

The Op-lite Company designed and produced one-of-a-kind lasers for special applications. The firm was not very profitable, and at one point a new vice president was brought in to try and straighten things out. The new vice president had little technical background in lasers, but he soon discovered that he could forecast the cost and completion dates of a project more accurately than the expert engineers. He simply looked over the past records and discovered that the engineers' estimates were consistently too low. He then developed a rough rule of thumb for increasing the estimates of time and money submitted to him and ended up with amazingly accurate forecasts.

Of course there are some of the expert's traits you cannot easily observe—namely, those that require an understanding of his special field. Nonetheless, there are a great many useful things you can learn about your expert. For example:

1. Does he tend to go too slowly or too quickly for you?
2. Does he tend to exaggerate or underplay the seriousness of a problem?
3. Does he get along well with others in the organization or tend to antagonize them?
4. Is he strong on diagnosis but weak on action (or the other way around)?
5. Is he better at details or at seeing the bigger picture?

Because there are always many things to learn about your expert, it's a good idea—if at all possible—to try him out first on a small project or a small piece of a major project. Such a pilot-project approach can help you and your expert get better acquainted with each other before the going gets too rough.

YOUR EXPECTATIONS

Many managers regard the expert as a "magic man" who will miraculously solve whatever problems he is handed. Unfortunately, most professional disciplines are much less powerful than they seem to those who aren't steeped in the particular field of knowledge. Managers realize that their own field of management is very imprecise, that management problems are very complex, that facts are often incomplete or highly uncertain. Yet the state of the art is not that much different in other fields, even in the so-called hard sciences.

A realistic set of expectations about a good expert might include the following:

1. The expert may discover that the problem is not what you thought it was.
2. The expert may uncover problems or complexities you did not know about.
3. The expert may have *ideas* about alleviating some of the problems, but he won't necessarily *solve* the problems.
4. The expert will help you analyze the pros and cons of various options and suggest additional alternatives, but you'll have to accept some of his opinions on faith, and to some degree the final decisions will still be up to you.

YOUR CONTRIBUTION

"The trouble with a specialist is that while he certainly has a place in the scheme of things, he just doesn't know the scheme."

I don't know who first concocted this caustic epithet, but it nicely captures the basic character of working with an expert. The expert has certain knowledge and skills but he doesn't know your situation. You know a lot about your situation but lack the skills and professional knowledge of the expert. If you're not going to pick up the expert's special knowledge and skills, then the expert will have to pick up a good deal about your situation; and the only way he can do this is from you or your people.

But there is still a basic dilemma: How do you know what to convey to the expert about your situation unless you're already an expert? Conversely, how can the expert know what is important about your situation unless he is already very familiar with it? Managers typically respond to this dilemma in one of two ways. Either they leave the expert on his own to "do his thing," or they try to set up rigorously detailed objectives that spell out exactly what they want.

Curiously enough, the risk of either approach is much the same: namely, that the expert will end up working on the wrong problem or objectives. If you leave the expert on his own, he's likely to guess poorly at what you really need or may end up working on what is most interesting to *him*. If you set up supposedly precise objectives, the expert may dutifully do what was prescribed—but there's a good chance that this won't lead to the results you really wanted or needed.

Okay, you have to start someplace, and the first move is usually up to you. So you expose the expert to as much of your situation as you think is relevant. It is, in fact, a good idea to outline roughly what you believe are your problems or objectives. But neither you nor your expert should be deluded into believing that you have told him all he needs to know, or that your statement of problems and objectives is completely accurate.

It is crucially important to realize, first, that *working with an expert is a joint effort* and, second, that *it requires a good deal of groping or muddling,* especially in the early stages. You and your expert need to check with each other continually to make sure you both stay on the same wavelength. All the caveats discussed in the preceding chapter on "Discretion" are doubly applicable in working with an expert.

In the process of muddling with your expert, *it is vital that you understand what he's talking about.* This may sound terribly obvious when stated this way, but when an expert talks about a "thriple sprotched fremish," many managers hesitate to ask for clarification. It is also surprising how many managers do not thoroughly read the memos, documents, or reports prepared for them by their experts. If the document is not written in a style you can understand, then it's up to you to ask the expert to explain it or write it in the form you desire. If there really is nothing of importance in the document, then it's up to you to help your expert spend his time more productively.

One of the most serious dangers in muddling with your expert is that in fact you end up second-guessing him. By second-guessing I mean pitting your limited knowledge of his field against his more complete knowledge. After all, the reason you hired the expert in the first place was that you needed his expertise. If you find yourself continually mistrusting his observations and opinions, then what you need is a different expert. *Second-guessing the expert you already have can only gum up the works.*

Now second-guessing is not the same as sharp questioning. For example, suppose a lawyer tells you that a particular customer contract requires you to provide certain materials at a much lower price than it now costs you to produce those materials. Second-guessing your lawyer would mean arguing with him about his legal interpretation of the contract (i.e., that the law obliges you to provide the materials at a fixed price even if your costs go up). Sharp questioning, on the other hand, might consist of asking him to support his conclusion in terms of relevant laws and legal precedents. You should certainly raise questions about how analogous the cases he cites are to your own. You should also ask him what possible loopholes he has checked out, and there's nothing wrong with your suggesting a few loopholes that have occurred to you. Perhaps you know something about the present situation that the lawyer is unaware of.

YOUR ATTITUDE

The more you look, the more you see—and often, the more you see, the more complex the world becomes. In a sense, an expert provides you with more "looking power," so the odds are that he will complicate your life rather than simplify it. The expert will make you aware of problems you didn't know you had; he will open up options you didn't think existed; he will generate new uncertainties; and he will push you into making difficult choices among conflicting values or objectives.

Overall you may be better off with an expert than without him, but your life will certainly not be any simpler. Among other things, your expert is likely to make you painfully conscious of just how much you are muddling. All this can make you feel upset, angry, or frustrated, and you have every right to those feelings. The danger is that you will vent such feelings on your expert when there is not much he can do about them. Even more hazardous is the chance that consciously or unconsciously you will press your expert to oversimplify by saying something like this: "All I want to know is whether we should sue or not. Now that's simple enough, isn't it?" Or like this: "Look, don't tell me all the 'ifs' and 'buts.' Just get the damn thing working." The risk in oversimplifying is that your expert will deliberately ignore important factors and make value decisions which are properly yours; and *you will never know it.*

Another important part of your attitude is the interest you take in what your expert is doing. Sure, an expert does get some intrinsic satisfaction just from being an expert and exercising his special skills. But experts, like everyone else, want to feel they're doing something useful and meaningful. If you don't provide the expert with this sort of payoff, he'll try to find it elsewhere. I don't mean he'll necessarily quit on you, but he may divert some of his energies from your priorities to ones which are more important to his personal or professional life (and he already has more than enough pressures in this direction anyway).

You may find that merely taking an active interest in what your expert is doing will prove a pleasant surprise to him, and will also prove a simple way to spur him on to greater efforts on your behalf. If your expert should turn out to be dedicated and competent in his work for you, it can't hurt for you to be grateful and proffer a warm "thank you." You may feel (even more than with a regular subordinate) that doing a good job is what the expert is paid for, but it certainly doesn't always turn out that way. Excellence in experts is just as rare as anywhere else.

Finally, in dealing with an expert it is well to remember that you're usually not the only client. Whether the expert is part of an internal service group in your organization or belongs to an outside firm, he's probably dealing with demands from a number of clients and must juggle his clients' priorities just like any other manager. The odds are that your projects won't always stay on top of the heap. In most cases, *you must resign yourself to the continuing need to expedite your expert's efforts.*

Expert Appraisal

All right, you've tried to pick a good expert and you didn't just drop it there. You expended considerable time and effort on muddling together with your expert. You still face, however, what is perhaps the most difficult task of all: evaluating him. At one point or another you'll have to make some judgment about your expert's abilities. For instance, your decision about whether or not to follow his recommendations will certainly depend in part on your confidence in him. Also, at the end of a project you must make a decision about whether or not to continue with the same expert on other tasks. Even before the end of a major project, there may be intermediate points at which you could choose to shift experts without creating too much havoc.

Appraising non-experts is hard enough, but the great difficulty in appraising an expert is that you can't pit your expertise against his. For example, his recommendations may be based on formulas you don't understand or research results you can't check. Inevitably, much of the expert's advice results from his feel for things (i.e., the application of his general background and experience), and that is difficult for you as a layman to dispute.

RATING RESULTS

Ask a manager how he judges the work of experts and the most common reply is, "by results." The expert gets the job done or he doesn't; his advice proves sound or it doesn't. Unhappily, this approach to evaluation is feasible in only a few situations— namely, where the expert over a short time span makes a number of small recommendations or decisions that create concrete, easily identifiable consequences. More often, however, the expert is dealing with complicated and uncertain situations. The effects of his advice or decisions become inseparably entangled with many other actions and events.

Frequently the results of an expert's work aren't visible for a very long time. It isn't much help to judge your insurance expert of five years ago incompetent after the plant has burned down and you find you weren't covered. It could be several years after your new computer is installed before you find out your expert recommended the wrong computer.

Thus, you must make tradeoffs between what is most relevant to evaluate and what is most feasible to evaluate. Results are surely relevant, but are often very difficult to observe or evaluate, at least in time to be of much use.

PERSONALITY IN THE PROFESSIONS

Personality is probably the most commonly used basis for evaluating experts, although managers may not like to admit it or may not even realize they are heavily relying on this basis. An expert's personality is something that is relatively easy to observe, and we all have pretty clear reactions to a personality.

But judging experts on the basis of personality can be very misleading. The problem is that we all tend to favor personalities that resemble our own. Yet the very fact that an expert has chosen a different profession from yours makes it likely that his personality will differ from yours.

Business professors Jay Lorsch and John Morse [1] have studied the character of different groups within an organization. They find that each functional group tends to have different predispositions. For example, scientists prefer autonomy, like to work alone, and are comfortable with ambiguity. By contrast, members of a manufacturing unit are predisposed to accept management control; they enjoy close working relationships with peers and do not tolerate ambiguity as well as scientists.

Of course, the personality of your expert is not totally irrelevant. Certainly if you feel your expert is a scoundrel or totally irresponsible, you ought to replace him. There is a difference, however, between liking your expert and being able to work with him. In any case, the point is that how much you like your expert may have little to do with his professional competence.

[1] Jay Lorsch and John Morse, *Organizations and Their Members* (New York: Harper & Row, 1974).

MONITORING METHODOLOGY

If observing results is impractical or impossible, and judging personality is irrelevant or unreliable, then on what basis can you evaluate an expert? I would suggest that "methodology" is about the best overall indicator of competence available to the layman; an expert's methodology is somewhat observable, judgeable, and relevant.

Of course, the more of an expert you are yourself, the more specifically you can judge an expert's methodology. But every manager has a good general idea of the methods involved in problem-solving, and problem-solving—in one form or another —is usually what an expert is hired to do. It is surprising how similar good methodology is in all specialties. What makes an expert unique is his ability to apply the general methodology to a specific kind of problem.

For example, *gathering information* is part of almost every problem-solving effort. No matter what kind of expert you're working with, you can check out how he went about gathering his data. To whom did he talk? What questions did he ask? What reports did he scan?

Diagnosis and evaluation are also key steps in most problem-solving, and good methodology implies a certain amount of care and thoroughness in these steps. How did the expert check the accuracy of his data? Does the diagnosis take account of all the relevant facts? What alternative diagnoses were suggested by the facts? What criteria were used in making the evaluation?

There is usually a *creative side* to working on many problems. How imaginative was the expert in coming up with alternative action possibilities? Did the expert play with different ways of defining the problem to see which was most useful?

Good methodology also involves *recognizing the limitations of the methodology* itself. Did the expert clarify the assumptions he made? Did he let you know what factors were being purposely ignored? Did he indicate what new conditions or contingencies would significantly alter his conclusions?

Problem prevention is perhaps just as important as problem-solving; problems are often much easier to handle in their early stages. A good expert will have paid some attention to uncovering possible problems—problems related to the ones you posed for him, and problems that may result from following his advice. The expert's advice should not just be a one-shot solution to the problem at hand; his advice should include ideas for avoiding or minimizing future problems of the same kind.

Now all this may sound a bit like a traditional treatise on rational problem-solving, but I don't mean to imply that your expert will actually do his work in such a rigorously logical way. Problem-solving of any kind is an art; more muddling and intuition than reason may be involved in arriving at conclusions. Much of what you're paying an expert for is precisely his ability to muddle in the area of his specialty. But as the expert's conclusions take shape he should be testing them for precision, consistency, and the additional criteria suggested in the preceding paragraphs.

It can be very difficult for you to share the expert's muddling and evaluate how he is working. But you certainly can and should participate with your expert in evaluating his output against the methodology of logical problem-solving. At the very least, then, you will realize to what degree your expert's work can be rationally supported and to what degree you will be flying with blind faith in his intuition and experience.

HOW MUCH HAVE YOU LEARNED?

There is one other factor you ought to include in your evaluation of your expert: *Has he taught you anything about his field of expertise* (other than how complicated and difficult it is)? You have many responsibilities for making an expert effective, but the expert has a few himself. One of his most important obligations is to educate you enough so that you can give him the appropriate input and understand most of his conclusions. Beware of the expert who shrouds everything in professional jargon, who keeps telling you everything is too complicated to explain. In particular, the expert should teach you something about the methods of his specialty (not necessarily how to apply them expertly). None of this will make you an expert or even a quasi-expert, but it is essential for working together effectively. If your expert doesn't provide such education, then perhaps he isn't the expert for you—even though he may otherwise be highly competent.

After the Evaluation

Of course, the risk of carefully evaluating your expert is that you may find him seriously deficient. You may shudder at the thought of again plunging into the arduous task of seeking a new expert, interviewing, breaking him in, and so forth. Your general reticence to fire anyone is probably stronger where an expert is concerned, if only because you may have less confidence in your evaluation.

True, some managers do hop from expert to expert in search of that ideal, nonexistent miracle worker, or in search of an expert who will agree with their own point of view. More often, the case is that managers don't change experts frequently enough. Over and over again a manager will return to use the same expert who was judged to be sadly lacking in the past. Even an expert who has turned in a good performance may not continue to do so forever. Experts can get bored, develop different interests, move into new specialties.

The choice is yours. No matter how you slice it, it's your money, or property, or people, or projects that the expert is handling.

Who's an Expert: A Final Fillip

Suppose you send one of your subordinates to check out some situation in another city or in some remote part of the organization. In a sense the subordinate becomes something of an expert; that is, he now knows a lot more about certain things than you do. If a subordinate performs a certain specialized task for several years, he also becomes a kind of expert—he has some skills and experience you do not have. In this light, it may be fair to say that many of your subordinates are experts.

In fact, since each of us has had unique experiences and possesses some unique capabilities, are we not all experts to each other? Aren't the problems of dealing with experts fundamental to the art of managing anybody? Are we not *all* managing from ignorance more than we may realize?

6:
LET'S GET TRAINING OUT OF THE HANDS OF TRAINERS

Dear Training Director:

Do the line managers regard your department as a bunch of fuzzy-headed interlopers?

Do you wonder why managers don't understand the importance of your training programs?

Are you tired of being low man on the organizational totem pole?

Is your budget among the first to be chopped when sales or profits drop?

If you answered YES to any of these questions, then you need our special "limited edition" report. This document is based on hundreds of contacts with large organizations and their training departments. The revolutionary ideas in this report are SIMPLE but POWERFUL; they will help you gain respect and results you never thought possible.

The confidential manuscript will not be reprinted once the current supply is exhausted. Orders will be filled on a first-come, first-served basis. So act promptly and get the jump on your counterparts in other organizations. The modest fee is FULLY REFUNDABLE within ten days of purchase if you don't feel the report is worth every penny of the price.

Simply fill out the enclosed coupon and attach your check for . . . .

Alas, this direct-mail campaign never reached the public. The whole project ran afoul of the law, apparently because of the full-color photograph on the cover of the report depicting a scantily clad female trainer providing instruction to a male executive wearing a very long tie and not much else. Perhaps the authorities felt the cover implied that training was to be given only to male managers and thereby violated equal-opportunity-employment laws; or perhaps the training techniques implied by the cover were simply considered too unorthodox.

In any case, I have obtained a copy of this provocative document through sources which I am not at liberty to reveal. The manuscript (which is now a collector's item) appears here in its full, uncut version—minus the controversial cover, which unfortunately had been torn off by someone before I received my copy.

CONFIDENTIAL REPORT TO TRAINING MANAGERS

There is no point in pussyfooting around until the last page to reveal the secret formula for success. It can all be summed up in a simple phrase: *Get training out of the hands of the trainers.* Don't panic. This report is not a detailed plan for committing departmental suicide. Actually, it is only by moving training into the hands of line managers that you can really hope to survive.

This report is marked "confidential" primarily to protect you from the misplaced reactions of your other training personnel. So far as the line managers go, should the manuscript fall into their hands the reaction will probably be "It's about time somebody suggested something like this." In fact, after you've read this report, you might "accidentally" leave it behind on the desk of one of your key operating vice presidents.

Just Like Planning and Budgeting

Why start out this report on training with a discussion of budgeting and planning? Because the development of the training function seems to be following tracks similar to those of budgeting and planning, yet budgeting and planning groups in most organizations presently have a legitimacy and impact far greater than that of the training department. Briefly tracing the evolution of budgeting and planning activities can help explain the present predicament of the training activity and why training is not yet as successful an activity as it could be.

The development of budgeting and planning in the United States can be broken down into essentially three phases. Of course, not all organizations go through the same phases at the same time. Moreover, budgeting provides an interesting contrast with planning because each is presently at a different phase of the cycle (though both are in a more advanced stage than training).

PHASE 1

The first phase is the "acquaintance" stage of the cycle. Books and articles are published describing the new technique, usually in terms of something akin to a miracle cure. Phase 1 typically includes a few experiments or pilot attempts to apply the new technique in a real organizational setting. The results are not always favorable.

Phase 1 for budgeting probably occurred in the 1920s, while for planning it didn't come until the 1950s.

PHASE 2

In the second phase, the new technique becomes a somewhat "legitimized" activity. Most organizations accept at least part of the technique as valid and feel compelled to give it a try. At first the new activity may be tacked onto an existing function, and later a separate group or department may be set up.

Thus, in the late 1940s many major corporations tried out some kind of formal budgeting. Budgeting groups were set up, typically as an adjunct to the accounting function. The planning activity followed a similar course a few decades later, in the 1960s. It was only toward the end of the sixties that any significant proportion of organizations had established formal, separate planning groups (and in many nonprofit organizations, such groups are only developing now).

Phase 2 was not a particularly happy time for the practitioners of budgeting or planning. Other managers in the organization felt these activities were unnecessary intrusions into the more important work at hand. Budgets were just a lot of paperwork shuffled around by those men with green eyeshades in the controller's department, and who knew what those pie-in-the-sky planners were up to?

In phase 2, top management did give some token notice that these new activities were important. So a manager tolerated the budget or planning people—as long as they didn't get in his hair too much. Budgeters and planners tended to pursue their own ways in semi-isolation, and the impact of their activities on the rest of the organization was minimal.

PHASE 3

A major characteristic of the third phase is the genuine (not token) interest and active support of top management—or at least, that's what most observers of the business scene have concluded in their many books and articles. Top management interest is prescribed as the basic answer to everything from improving the use of the computer to better motivation; from raising environmental quality to improving safety standards. Certainly little can be accomplished without the support (or at least the acquiescence) of top management. By itself, however, top management support is usually not sufficient to move an activity into phase 3.

The key to phase 3 is *to move the activity into the hands of the line managers;* that is, the new function must become an integral part of a line manager's activity. All too often top management support is directed solely at encouraging the special little group charged with the new activity. In fact, sometimes giving the special group more funds and manpower or the status of titles and big offices just encourages the group to remain isolated.

Today, budgeting is in phase 3. Oh, budgets are still the butt of many jokes and the bane of some managers' existence. Yet few managers would agree to run a department without using some form of budgeting. The arguments center on *how the budget should function, not on the basic usefulness of a budget.*. The battles rage over what the numbers in a budget should be, not whether such numbers are needed.

The differences between phase 2 and phase 3 are more dramatically illustrated in the planning area, because the transition is going on right now. In the late sixties the management literature trumpeted forth the need for top management support of and involvement in the planning function. Slowly, some top managements began to provide such support, and a few even made the head of planning a vice president. The planning departments grew larger and the plans thicker, but often the impact of formal planning was minimal. Some plans turned out to require resources and abilities for their implementation that simply did not exist within the organization. In other cases, the detailed plans were simply ignored.

A large manufacturer of industrial equipment did an elaborate analysis of future technological and market developments. The study highlighted several weak areas that needed bolstering. At the time, however, the company was engaged in a critical cost-cutting program, negotiating several important acquisitions, and revising its distribution system. The planning vice president fought the good fight, but the studies ended up moldering away in a locked file drawer.

In the early 1970s, something called management by objectives caught on (although the basic terms and concepts had been around for more than a decade). The key concept of MBO was that each manager was to get together with his subordinates and work out mutually-agreed-upon objectives against which the subordinate would be evaluated. A great many organizations set up formal MBO programs, and many others adopted much the same approach without formally calling it MBO. Notice that the key thing about the MBO kind of approach is that it begins to involve every manager in planning.

What Phase Is Training In?

Nowadays almost nobody is against training. Few top managements would contemplate taking a serious public stand against management development. It is generally accepted that people don't always come with all the requisite skills; managers and other employees must be developed. The pace of change and innovation is accelerating. Continuing education is touted as essential, just to keep up with all the changes; it is increasingly talked about as part of the self-fulfillment to which every manager is entitled.

The dollars are flowing, although accurate figures are hard to come by. A 1974 Hope Report [1] estimates that $11 billion is spent on training annually (although that figure includes the salaries of the learners during the time they're not on the job). IBM, General Motors, Xerox, the U.S. Civil Service Commission, and many other large organizations have set up their own school facilities for management training. Few large organizations are without a training department of some sort. Certainly training is no longer in phase 1.

The support of top management for training, however, is often not a profound commitment but more a thin veneer of tokenism—a characteristic of phase 2. While the dollars do flow for training, the tap is quickly turned down at the hint of any slowdown in business. For instance, in early 1975 a *Business Week* article observed:

> . . . in today's recession, management development programs, which are supposed to provide in-depth backup at every level and facilitate the transfer of power at the top, are on nearly every corporate cost cutter's list.[2]

Typically the head of a training department is two or three levels below a vice president. Even when there's a vice president for training, he's generally the lowest-paid vice president on the organizational roster.

For their part, many managers are at best apathetic toward the various training programs available to them in their organ-

---

[1] *Industry: AV and Training,* vol. 3 (Rochester, N.Y.: Thomas W. Hope Reports, Inc., February 1974).
[2] "How Companies Raise a New Crop of Managers," *Business Week,* March 10, 1975.

ization (another characteristic of phase 2). They may be enthusiastic if invited to attend a special seminar where attendance is considered a treat or is a signal that the manager is in line for a promotion. More often, however, a manager knows he's being sent to a training course because he has a bit of spare time between assignments, or as a last-ditch effort to save him from being fired or demoted. A top executive of one major oil and gas well tool company put it this way: "I send a guy to school when he's screwed up and I want to get him out of my hair."

When a manager returns from a two-day seminar, he's typically greeted with comments like these:

> Well, I guess you enjoyed the vacation; now let's get back down to work!

> Welcome back to the world of reality. Hope you didn't take those dewy-eyed training types too seriously.

In other words, if the *concept* of training is held in high repute, trainers and their actual training activities are not.

Most line managers do participate in some form of training, but primarily as students. Training is clearly not yet in the hands of the managers. It's still in phase 2, and few trainers or anyone else seem to have seriously contemplated the desirability of moving it into phase 3.

The Trouble with Training

So what if training is in phase 2? Just because budgeting and planning moved into a third phase, why should training follow the same path? To answer these questions, it's first necessary to dig a little deeper into the current problems in training.

TRAINING VERSUS MANAGERS' PROBLEMS

Ask a harried line manager what's on his mind and the answer may sound something like this (with expletives deleted):

> Well, I guess the major crisis is that we're behind schedule, and in addition our costs are really getting out of hand. The whole thing is going to get worse if I don't get this flap with the marketing people ironed out.

Now on top of all of this I've got to get in my projections for the next six months, which also means sitting down with my people and working out some reasonable targets.

Which reminds me, I also have to get moving on a replacement for one of my key people who left last week. And, oh yes, my boss is pressuring me to get back to him with my comments on the new product specs.

I guess I sure picked the wrong time to add some items to our paperwork reporting system, because it looks like it's going to take a lot of my time to iron out all the bugs.

Now take the above examples of what might be on a manager's mind and set them down next to a typical list of training courses (a rarely made comparison, by the way). On the left are the various "typical" problems extracted from the manager's monologue. On the right is a list of training courses offered by the training department of a well-known Midwestern corporation selling high-priced industrial equipment.

Items on the Manager's Mind	*Training Courses*
Catch up on schedule; i.e., more output	Problem-Solving
	Line-Staff Workshop
Cut costs	Motivation
Flap with marketing department	Time Resource Management
	Management by Objectives
Six-month projection	Recruiting Skills
Goals for my staff	Conference Leadership
Replace key person	Better Listening
Comment on new product	Financial Management for
Change paperwork system	Nonfinancial Managers
	Transactional Analysis

One problem is immediately apparent: For the most part it doesn't look as if the training packages are really going to help the manager solve his problems. No wonder the manager feels apathetic.

Of course, as a training manager you may have come to exactly the opposite conclusion. For instance, wouldn't the line-staff workshop help the manager work through his problems with the marketing department? Wouldn't the motivation course help him cut costs and get more output from his people, and wouldn't it probably be pertinent to setting staff goals? Wouldn't the problem-solving course be likely to apply to every one of the items on the manager's list?

Okay, Mr. Training Director, your courses may indeed be relevant to what's on a manager's mind. But by and large, *no one course is sufficient to help the manager with any one particular problem.* Even all the courses together may not really provide what a manager needs to cope with a specific problem. There are, of course, a few exceptions on the training list (there always are). For instance, the manager may believe (or find out) that "Management by Objectives" is directly related to his need for setting staff goals, or that "Recruiting Skills" could help him find the key employee he's looking for.

To put it another way, the manager's list tends to state things in terms of "outputs"—that is, tasks for which he is responsible (whether he does them himself or gets them done through others). Accomplishment of these tasks is what the manager feels he is paid to do, what he will incur penalties for failure to perform. The more tangible or measurable the task, the more likely he is to be judged by it. What the manager sees as problems are those things which seem to stand in the way of his accomplishing such tasks.

The list of training courses is more oriented toward "skills" than "outputs." Certainly, many of these skills are needed or relevant for the accomplishment of tasks facing the manager; they can help overcome some of the barriers. Generally, however, there is no one-to-one correspondence between a given skill (training course) and a specific task or problem facing a manager. The manager is interested in getting results, taking action, making decisions, or solving problems. He is not interested in acquiring skills per se. No wonder the manager tends to see the trainer as an outsider who doesn't really understand his problems.

TRAINING'S VIEW OF HOW TO MANAGE

If the manager and the trainer organize their interests differently, then the split is widened by a fundamental difference between the way managers manage and the trainer's view of the management process. Behind the precise, neat façade of budgets, objectives, and computer printouts lurks a managerial world filled with ambiguity, complexity, and uncertainty. Deep down, every manager senses this fuzzy, confusing character of organizational life. He also knows from sad experience that hard-nosed analysis has only limited power for coping with the chaotic character of his environment. Much of the time a manager must muddle.

Most training packages, however, ignore both the fuzzy nature of the manager's world and the muddling approach so necessary for successfully operating in that world. Training sessions tend to present neat, logical prescriptions or conceptual schemes which the manager finds very difficult to apply to his real problems. Of course the manager probably doesn't enjoy muddling, so he may be quite enthusiastic about the prospect of receiving a nice "how to" list. Yet he will naturally find any specific prescription or list somewhat unrealistic or impractical, and will end up grumbling about the ivory-tower approach of the training department.

TRAINING AND TRANSLATION

If managers muddle, then each manager muddles somewhat differently because of his own special background, experience, and abilities. If each manager confronts a fuzzy world around him, then that world is somewhat different for each manager. Each person has a different list of problems on his mind, and even the same problem may appear quite different to different people.

Training attempts to change the trainee in some way. But new knowledge or skill does not create much change unless it is somehow assimilated into the person's unique environment. The "glob" of knowledge has to be connected up—that is, linked to—

the special world in which the person moves and hooked into what the person already knows. I use the term "translation" to refer to this integration process—a process which involves much more than mere intellectual acquaintance with some new knowledge or skill.

Effecting a knowledge transplant is nearly as tricky as performing a kidney transplant: Rejection of alien matter is a problem that looms large in both processes. Successful translation inevitably involves adapting the glob of knowledge or skill so that it can survive in its new environment, so that the necessary life-giving connections can be made. Changes must also be made in the environment to which the knowledge is transplanted; that is, some of the already-existing connections may have to be modified or broken to accommodate the new glob of knowledge or skill. This is what translation is all about.

Training (like most other forms of teaching) often ignores the problems of translation, or assumes them away by putting the burden of translation entirely on the learner. Many a weary teacher consoles himself by claiming, "All we can do is explain the thing clearly; the rest is up to the student." Other, more caustic trainers have been heard to mumble a modified version of a well-known saying: "You can lead a manager to knowledge, but you can't make him think."

Even the highly touted "case method" of instruction does not really cope with the problems of translation. Typically the "case" is used to point up important principles and knowledge. Sometimes the case is used as a specific context in which the learner can practice applying new knowledge or skills. The idea is that if the case process is repeated using many cases, then the student will have learned to make the proper translation into any situation.

The problem, however, is that none of the case situations are part of the learner's real environment. Ironically, this characteristic of the case method is supposed to be one of its virtues. The argument is that a case puts a certain distance between the learner and his own real-life activities. Thus the learner can look at new ideas more objectively, free from the politics, emotional commitments, and biases involved in his immediate problems.

While the concept of distancing may be very helpful in the acquaintance phase of learning, it is a move away from the crucial process of translation. The case situation simply does not portray the actual environment of the trainee, which is why managers tend to complain about cases that don't deal with the same industry and product as their own.

Moreover, the trainee is not really a character in the case; he only pretends to be. He tries to decide what he would do *if* he were the decision-making character, *if* he were in the case situation. In discussing a case, the trainee can easily avoid doing much translation. As many hard-nosed executives are fond of pointing out, there is an enormous difference between the steps you take to meet a payroll in real life and what you contemplate doing in a case, or between firing a real person and firing someone in a case.

Students in the ivied groves of academe seem willing to tolerate a teacher's lack of attention to translation. But managers have a job to do, and they demand that training provide some *direct* assistance to *them* on *specific* problems right *now*. Note that on-the-job training does usually deal with some of the problems of translation. It is probably no coincidence that most recent surveys of training indicate that on-the-job training is the most widely used and is thought to be the most effective type of training. In any case, trainers' lack of attention to translation certainly contributes to the typical manager's adverse attitude.

TRAINING IS A "ONE-NIGHT AFFAIR"
(or a couple of days at most)

Real learning is more like a marriage than a one-night affair. Suppose the trainee returns from a good training session, sincerely committed to some new ideas or ways of thinking, packed full of brave new resolutions. Alas, the rest of his environment is not much different from what it was when he left it.

Subordinates, bosses, deadlines, and all the other pressures continue in their old ways. Moreover, when the trainee discusses his new ideas, he may find that people don't understand what he's talking about (another part of the translation problem). The forces in the outside environment provide little sustenance for the trainee's fragile new connections. The new roots are likely to be crushed out of existence before they've really taken hold, as the trainee quickly retreats to his more established methods of coping with problems. This fade-out phenomenon is well known to almost every teacher. The education literature incessantly harps on the need for reinforcement. Training sessions often do provide reinforcement—during the session, *but not afterwards*.

Translation takes time: time for new habits to develop, time to gain experience and confidence in the new learning. Without follow-up and continued reinforcement, the training session quickly recedes into obscurity with only a little glow (or sometimes a slight burning sensation) to remind the trainee of his "brief encounter." And what of the trainer? He feels frustrated, and firmly resolves to do better at the next one-night stand.

WHAT'S IN IT FOR THE TRAINEE?

No matter how good the trainer or the materials, no matter how much attention is paid to translation, no matter how much follow-up is provided, it will all come to naught if the trainee does not desire to learn. Some of the motivation for learning can come from the trainee's desire for self-improvement, his wish to expand his horizon, his interest in achieving increased understanding of the world around him. Amidst the pressures of organization life, however, there must usually be other incentives as well.

Unfortunately, most organizations provide few incentives for training other than verbal encouragement. The figures on which managers are judged usually do not include anything related to training. Overall organization plans generally pay little attention to the activity of training. Raises or promotions are generally not tied to training in any direct way, nor are the more informal types of recognition such as a bigger office, assignment of desired tasks, or inclusion in important meetings. Certainly as it now stands, the training department is relatively powerless to provide much in the way of direct incentives for training.

Why Move Training into the Hands of the Managers?

For each of the troubles with training discussed in the preceding section, let us now briefly examine what needs to be done to improve the situation.

RELEVANCE

Every marketing manager worth his salt knows how important it is to get to know the customer and determine what is important to that customer. Yet salesmen probably spend a great deal more time with their customers than the training department spends with its "customers," and a company generally shapes its products or services with more input from its consumers than the training department gets from its "consumers." You can't just chat with a customer once in a while or periodically have him fill out a questionnaire (which may not even ask the right questions).

Trainers don't get to know their manager-customers nearly as well as they should. They need to get a feel for the kinds of problems on the manager's mind, the nature of the disordered world in which he lives, and the muddling process required to cope with this fuzzy world and its attendant problems. It is simply not enough for a trainer to gather a list of problems from a manager, or to try to introduce some techniques for muddling during the course of a seminar. Somehow the managers themselves must become more directly involved in the processes of designing and even presenting training materials. Such an approach is in fact being used more and more by the so-called organizational development (OD) groups. It is interesting to note that these OD groups also tend to present themselves as "problem-solvers," not bearers of training.

Of course you could argue that the relevance problem might also be solved by somehow making the line managers "see the light"—that is, realize the relevance of the existing training materials to their problems. This pious hope still burns bright in the soul of many a trainer. But what will cause this enlightenment to take place? The managers' attitudes won't shift miraculously of their own accord. One answer would be a specific type of training designed to help a manager understand why the existing training materials are really relevant to his problems—in other words, training about training. But isn't this again a form of moving training more into the hands of the managers?

TRANSLATION

Suppose that somehow you could get all the managers to realize the relevance of the existing training materials. The problems of translation must still be tackled. If a trainer could deal with just a few managers over an extended period of time, then theoretically he might learn how to provide much of the necessary translation. The cost of such an approach, however, makes it no more than a seductive pipe dream. An organization has hundreds of managers whose problems change constantly from year to year and even from week to week. Few trainers can hope

to comprehend fully the specific fuzzy world and muddling of a given manager.

Inevitably it will be the manager who shoulders the major burden of making the necessary translation, if translation is going to occur at all. Certainly a manager may need to be made more aware of the translation process; he might well need some guidance with a specific translation problem. But somehow the manager's own knowledge of his problems and people must become more intimately involved *in the training process,* or else there will be little translation.

REINFORCEMENT

The problems of follow-up and reinforcement essentially boil down to a matter of manpower. Even the sizable training staffs of some large organizations come nowhere near reaching 100 percent of the employees or managers in a given year. The manpower bind becomes immediately apparent by making these rough calculations:

The 1,250 largest businesses in the United States have an average of about 20,000 employees. One day of training a month for groups of 10 employees would require *the full-time efforts of approximately 200 trainers* in each organization. (This assumes one hour of preparation, scheduling, and administrative time for each hour of actual training.) Designing and developing course materials would require considerable manpower in addition to the staff of 200.

The moral is that line managers are the only hope for providing the necessary follow-up and continuous reinforcement on which the success of training depends. It is the line managers who are in daily contact with their subordinates and peers, not the trainers. It is the continued presence of the manager on the scene that provides the only feasible opportunity for both formal and informal reinforcement of training.

CONTROLS AND INCENTIVES

The training department might devise reporting and planning systems that would include more attention to the training activity. The trainers might develop various incentives and controls to reward people for participating in training. But essentially it is only operating management which can decide to implement such measures. Only if training is truly in the hands of the managers is it likely that the necessary incentives and controls for training will creep into the system.

In summary, it looks—on almost all counts—as if the troubles with training will persist as long as training gets done exclusively by trainers. This point of view is not totally novel. Over ten years ago, Harold Wolff (a management consultant with Booz, Allen & Hamilton) carefully analyzed the success of the General Motors Corporation.[3] Wolff convincingly argued that the organization and financial techniques described by Alfred Sloan (and many others) were not sufficient to explain GM's success. Wolff concluded that the real secret was the attention and involvement of operating executives in the development of managerial talent. He found that GM executives generally agreed that they spent at least as much time on the problem of developing the management skills of their subordinates as they did on problems of production or sales. As one GM executive put it: "Executives of other companies who visit GM are always amazed to find how much time each GM executive spends on this single problem of building the management competence of our organization at every level of the company."[4]

The *Business Week* study cited previously (p. 130) found certain common threads running through the programs considered most effective. Besides unwavering top management support and long-term commitment, two other factors were mentioned:

1. [The programs] are built deep into the system, involving all levels of management and affecting the way the organization works.

2. Management development is part of every manager's job. Each executive is responsible for grooming his subordinates, and his salary and promotions are based partly on their success.[5]

[3] Harold A. Wolff, "The Great GM Mystery," *Harvard Business Review,* September–October 1964.
[4] Quoted in ibid.
[5] "How Companies Raise a New Crop of Managers," op. cit.

However, even those few companies that try to involve all managers in the *development* process seem to overlook the importance of actually engaging managers in the *formal training* activity. For instance, a major oil company emphasizes the following points in describing the involvement of its managers:

1. Management development is closely scrutinized from the top via an eight-person committee of inside directors.
2. Each major operating unit has its own committee for reviewing fast-rising managers.
3. Each line manager draws up a long-range plan for the replacement needs of his group, and the plan includes an appraisal of all his key executives. All the plans are then reviewed at various higher levels.

This description is typical of many others in its focus on manpower planning and appraisal activities and lack of emphasis on deep involvement in the training process itself.

The one place in which there seem to be signs of real interest in phase 3 training is in the *marketing* departments of several large corporations. (Of course, a great many corporations already use special marketing staff trainers rather than central training department personnel to do the sales training.) At IBM, for instance, branch managers have actually been used as the leaders for certain sales training programs (some five programs in eighteen months). For each program the branch manager spent two days going through the program and then two days in presenting the program to his people.

No doubt, however, you're still concerned about what moving training into the hands of managers might really mean for managers as well as for trainers. The final sections of this confidential report provide some glimpses of what phase 3 for training might be like.

Managers as Trainers

There is a joker in the deck. *Training is already in the hands of managers,* and has always been there. The dictionary defines the verb "teach" like this: "to show or demonstrate; give instructions to; provide with knowledge or insight; cause to know or understand." Thus, in the broadest sense of the term, a manager is probably teaching any time he communicates with someone else, be it his boss, his subordinates, or managers in other departments. More specifically, a manager is continuously providing on-the-job training, sometimes formally and the rest of the time informally. Certainly when the manager is explaining what he wants and how he wants it done, he is training. Supervision, follow-up, and even evaluation are all ways in which a manager teaches his subordinates. Moreover, what a manager does on his own inevitably serves to instruct his subordinates—that is, do as I do, not as I say. In an organization people learn primarily from doing, and perhaps the most effective form of training is doing under the guidance of a "master doer."

Thus, phase 3 for training primarily means forcing managers to formally recognize and execute a responsibility which has been inescapably theirs all along.

IT'S NOT MY JOB

If training is already in the hands of managers, most of them neither realize it nor want it. Look at any of the standard lists of managerial functions. The task of teaching is nowhere to be found. Oh yes, those lists usually do include something like "developing subordinates," but that is interpreted to mean training them for bigger responsibilities—some job other than the one they're doing now.

A subordinate is supposed to know how to do his job, right? Isn't that what delegation is all about? Training seems to be something a manager "shouldn't ought to have to do." No doubt the manager's boss feels much the same way, and therefore does not provide the manager with much incentive to worry about training. Training becomes an unwelcome obligation that feels like a diversion of a manager's time and energy from the important work at hand.

Often the existence of a training department only reinforces the manager's dream of spending little time as a trainer himself. To remedy the unfortunate "deficiencies" of his subordinates, all the manager has to do is ship them off to a few sessions run by the training department.

Even if a manager accepts the burden of training, he may be quite unsure what to do. Most managers have spent from 12 to 20 years of their lives in school, watching teachers in action. Yet probably *not one day of that schooling was ever devoted to learning about teaching.* In other words, most managers have received little explicit training about training.

It may be that a manager avoids taking responsibility for training because he really doesn't know how to provide it, or because he feels training is something he shouldn't have to do. In either case, the manager ends up frustrated; the realities of his job make him a trainer whether he likes it or not.

RECOGNIZING REALITY

If training is already in the hands of managers and must remain there, then what phase 3 would do is formally recognize and deal with this situation. Phase 3 would legitimize the training part of a manager's job: All managers would be expected to devote a certain part of their time to training, just as it is now expected that they devote time to budgeting and planning. Managers would be held responsible for the effectiveness of their training, just as they are now held responsible for the caliber of their budgeting and planning activities.

Of course there will be problems; but there already are. And at least the problems will be out in the open where they can be worked at. Sure, skill in training is not the easiest thing in the world to measure or evaluate, but then neither are delegation, supervision, planning, and the other skills on which a manager is currently judged. Certainly managers will not become expert trainers overnight. When budgeting or planning moved into the hands of managers, special efforts were required to help managers develop the necessary new skills. Naturally some managers will prove better at training than other managers, but you can make the same statement about any managerial skill.

Another, more serious problem would result from the tendency of teaching to expose what the teacher doesn't know. It's very difficult to teach someone something when you don't know what you're talking about. If managers became more formally involved in actual training, many of them would feel quite uncomfortable about publicly displaying their ignorance. Some might even decide to bone up on what they're already supposed to know. Budgeting and planning also tend to point up what a manager doesn't know about his operation—which, by the way, accounts for much of the remaining resistance toward these activities. But managers do budget and plan. They do put in the required homework, and they're generally regarded as better managers because of it.

TIME FOR TRAINING

Training takes time; there's no way around it. If a manager can get what he wants without training, then there's no time problem (and no training problem). But if training is really necessary, then the time has to be spent—by somebody. All the facts suggest that the manager would be a much more efficient source of training than the training department, and in many cases more effective as well.

It boils down to a question of organization policy. Budgeting and planning also take up some of the manager's nonexistent spare time. But the top management of many organizations deems these activities important enough to have some of the available man-hours spent on them. If the true cost of effective training is found to be too high for the expected benefits, then at least top management can make a rational decision to dispense with the training effort and save the money wasted on dabbling with training that is not really productive.

What's to Become of Trainers?

Have no fear. Even if the managers are doing most of the training, the training department will not disappear. Phase 3 has not caused the demise of budgeting and planning groups; if anything, it has caused these groups to expand much more rapidly than they did in phase 2. The character and activities of the training department, however, would radically change in phase 3.

In phase 3 the training department would become primarily

a key source of expertise for helping managers to do the training. Again, the parallel with budgeting and planning groups is illuminating. For instance, in phase 3 a planning group actually helps managers improve their planning. A planner may sit down with a manager and help him define or clarify his objectives and discuss setting up appropriate milestones. The planner may help the manager assess his progress in implementing the plans and even suggest the possibility of revisions from time to time. The planner may also introduce new techniques for planning to the manager, or bring him up to date on the latest wrinkles in forecasting. So in phase 3 the trainer will help the manager with his training in much the same ways.

TRAINING ABOUT TRAINING

If managers do much of the training, trainers would still have the task of training people about the learning process. The trainer would help the manager discover both how he himself learns and how his subordinates learn (including the ways in which subordinates learn things the manager would prefer they didn't). The trainer would attempt to increase the manager's repertory of teaching techniques as well as to broaden his awareness of the techniques he already uses (often unconsciously).

No doubt trainers would supervise and monitor some of the manager's formal training sessions, and possibly even some of his more informal training. In a sense the trainer would become a consultant to the manager: The trainer would discuss the manager's problems with him, advise him about the appropriate kind of training, and then help assemble the appropriate training packages for him to use.

Who knows, this somewhat new role for trainers might even provide them with a greater understanding and tolerance for those "stubborn, narrow-minded managers" out there, while the managers might come to appreciate the usefulness of those "fuzzy-headed training types."

CURRICULUM DESIGN

The designing of effective training materials requires special skills quite different from those involved in being an effective seminar leader or teacher. Even now this split is recognized in most training departments, where only a few of the trainers are actually involved in designing courses. In phase 3 the design function would probably still remain primarily within the training department, although the managers would be much more involved in determining the content of the training materials than they were in phase 2.

Again the situation would be akin to what has happened in budgeting and is now occurring with planning. The budgeting group has the special skills to develop appropriate budget formats, just as the planning group evolves the structure for laying out plans. The very fact that managers must supply most of the content for budgets and plans and then use them in their work forces the designers to become more aware of the manager's needs and problems. A similar change in the orientation of designers could be expected in phase 3 for training.

DIFFERENT TECHNIQUES FOR TRAINING

It is hard to foresee exactly what new techniques phase 3 would bring to training, but some of the possibilities are already on the horizon. For instance, programmed instruction will certainly prove useful in phase 3, but the trend may be more toward what might be called broad-band programming. Training materials developed for sale by Columbia Pictures, Tratec, Xerox, and others already involve significant departures from the small-step–by–small-step programmed instruction of the past. Broad-band programming can allow learners to relate the material more directly to their own problems and still stay on the programming "track." The pioneer efforts in this direction also indicate that highly structured (i.e., programmed) materials can be used effectively in groups rather than for individual study alone. The discussions that occur within the group, of course, add significantly to the value of the training.

Another possible development is the emergence of various forms of "learner-aided" instruction. As training moves into the hands of managers, there will be more emphasis on translation and on making direct use of the learning. Since to some degree it is only the learners who can make the final translation, why not give them more control over the training process itself? Robert Mager has already done some intriguing experiments along this line. For instance, in a course for training engineers, he allowed the trainees to determine the sequencing of the learning. Training time was significantly reduced, including the total time demands on the teacher.[6]

Peter Rosenbaum of Teachers College in New York City has conducted widespread experiments with another type of learner-aided instruction which he calls "peer-mediated instruction" (PMI). In essence PMI is a somewhat sophisticated version of the old "buddy system." Rosenbaum prestructures the sequence and content of the course, but it is the learners who actually help teach the material to each other.

As the role of a formal course changed, so would its content. For example, training would probably become heavily *project-related;* that is, as a manager and his people worked on a real-life problem they would uncover the need for certain information or new skills. At such a point there would be true motivation for training, and the help of a training expert might be very welcome. Together, the manager and trainer could map out an appropriate program. The trainer could then help the manager assemble the needed instructional materials. To a large degree the trainer would thus be forced into the fuzzy world of the manager and would help the manager with his muddling through.

Because passive understanding is rarely enough to generate real changes in thinking or behavior, at some point the trainee must be given an opportunity to try out his new skill or knowledge. The trainee needs to get a feel for what the change is like and how it might work for him; he must experiment. But experiments of this kind in the real world can seem very risky. Thus an important part of project-related training would be *the design of*

---

[6] Robert F. Mager, "Learner Controlled Instruction—1958–1964." *Programmed Instruction,* Vol. 4, No. 2 (New York: The Center for Programmed Instruction of the Institute of Educational Technology, Teachers College, Columbia University, November 1964).

special experiments in settings that are safe enough and loose enough to encourage trying out new ideas. At other times a highly controlled form of experiment may be needed, in which careful consideration is given to what is to be tried out, for how long, and how results are to be evaluated. In phase 3, the professional trainer would assist the manager in designing and implementing the various experiments needed to convert new knowledge and skills into actual changes in on-the-job behavior.

JOB ROTATION

AT&T and a few other companies have tried the approach of rotating various line managers through the training function; that is, they assign a few line managers to a tour of duty in the training department for a year or two. The idea is that over the years, a number of managers will be exposed (or subjected) to the training point of view while at the same time the managers will force the trainers to face up to the harsher realities of life on the firing line.

These rotation schemes generally have not been very successful. While the line manager is exposed to the training gospel, he rarely gets religion (if only because he knows he'll soon be back in the saddle again). Often, all the manager ends up with is a smattering of the training jargon. Moreover, the manager finds he can exert little influence on the professional trainers (if only because they view him as a non-expert who will be moving on shortly). The trainers find they can safely ignore the opinions of the manager-in-training.

So long as training remains in phase 2, neither the trainers nor the managers have much incentive to make such a job-rotation program meaningful. Once the decision is firmly made to move training into the hands of the managers, however, the ball game changes and rotation programs could be very productive. Of course at that point it could be just as important for trainers to work a while at nontraining jobs as it would be for managers to spend time in the training department. Perhaps the Chinese are way ahead of the United States in forcing all their teachers to work a while in the farm fields.

BROADER HORIZONS

During phase 2, the training department must continually fight to justify its own existence. Often this leads trainers to act as if training were some kind of an ultimate end in itself, which of course irritates managers, who don't see it that way.

As training moves into the hands of managers, the managers would naturally become more aware of what training can do and when it is useful. They would soon realize that almost any major organizational change requires many employees to develop new skills and new ways of thinking or behaving. *Training can play a key role in the effective implementation of new policies* as diverse as centralization of the purchasing function, a new fringe-benefit program, and automation of a production line. Once more, the parallel with budgeting and planning is instructive. These functions—in organizations where they have reached phase 3— tend to be intimately involved in the development and implementation of almost every major new program or policy.

The more managers become immersed in teaching and learning, the more activities they will find that involve some kind of training. For instance, new product bulletins, reports to stockholders, and meetings with security analysts all involve teaching and learning. Firms in the auto, business equipment, pharmaceuticals, and many other industries that have set up video cassette networks have already found that these networks are beginning to blur the distinctions between training and many other forms of communication.

Nobody Said It Would Be Easy

Change is always difficult, particularly when you're involved in the change yourself. New skills and attitudes do not develop overnight, and moving training into the hands of managers means plenty of change for both managers and trainers. Managers will resent taking on yet another responsibility, even though they do in fact already have it. Trainers who only know how to run seminars will fear for their jobs, even though those jobs may already be on a shaky basis (because the results of training are so minimal).

The prospects for change, however, are not all on the gloomy side. After all, similar changes did somehow take place in the field of budgeting and are now taking place in the activity of planning. Already a major soap and cosmetics firm, a large metal products company, and several other corporations have taken the first few conscious steps toward putting training into the hands of managers. For many years most major corporations in Japan have conducted continuous weekly training sessions for almost all employees—sessions typically run by supervisors and other line employees, not professional trainers.

The fascinating thing is that neither trainers nor managers need wait for a top management decision to move training into phase 3. Any trainer or manager who is so inclined can take certain steps toward phase 3, without elaborate plans and permissions and without requiring that the changes be made throughout the whole organization. Certainly a top management decision to formally move training into the hands of the managers would be of enormous help. But for the time being, all a trainer needs to do is find an interested manager (or vice versa) and go to it on his own.

If you have read this far and still find yourself against moving training into phase 3, then the question you must ask yourself is how long training can survive if it doesn't make such a change. In an era that portends increasing scarcity of resources, how long will management find it fashionable to spend huge sums on an activity with apparently meager benefits? How long can training departments survive in the current atmosphere of apathy or outright hostility directed toward them by the rest of the organization? Are you better off resisting any move to phase 3 or helping to shape the movement? When you come right down to it, you don't have much to lose by taking the lead in getting training out of the hands of trainers, and you have much to gain.

7:
THE FUZZY SIDE
OF MANAGEMENT:
An Introduction

Logicians have but ill defined
  as rational, the human kind.
Reason they say belongs to man;
But let them prove it if they can.
JONATHAN SWIFT
The Logicians Refuted (1731)

That there is a fuzzy side to management helps explain why
management often isn't the way it's "supposed to be"; and why, if
management can be better than it is, improvement often lies in a very
different direction than is commonly assumed.

This message is what this book is about. Each chapter ex-
amines the relationship of the message to a particular kind of
activity or context. This chapter talks about the message itself,
in a more general setting. Thus it is a kind of introduction, but
had it come at the start I fear it might have seemed simply too
. . . well . . . fuzzy.

Managerial Modes

Much of managerial thinking is presumed to involve analysis and
logic—that is, the reasoning mode. Other kinds of thinking are
usually thrown into the category of intuition—sometimes called
instinct, feeling, or hunch. Yet my observations indicate that
managers spend a good deal of time operating in still a third
mode—a mode that cannot truly be classified as either intuiting
or reasoning. This third mode is what in previous chapters I have
called "muddling."

152

INTUITING

This mode will be discussed first only because there is relatively little to say about it. I see intuiting as a kind of direct knowing or understanding that occurs in the unconscious mind. It is only certain results of the intuiting process that are available to consciousness for further consideration. Is the intuitive process emotional or nonlogical or what? I find it fruitless to pursue this kind of question very far. If intuiting is unconscious thinking, then not much more can be said about it. As I define it, the unconscious represents a sort of inaccessible black box whose inner workings are forever sealed from prying eyes; we cannot know exactly what the unconscious is or how it is operating. Our inability to describe unconscious processes, however, does not render them any less (or more) real and useful.

It is true that over the years we have developed the ability to control consciously certain forms of thinking which at one time might have been considered intuitive. Many forms of psychotherapy attempt to generate exactly such developments in the individual patient. In a similar vein, we are discovering that we have the ability to control certain bodily functions (such as blood pressure or body temperature) that were previously thought to be not subject to voluntary control. I don't think, however, that these newly controllable elements should continue to be lumped with those processes which still remain in the uncontrollable domain that is our unconscious.

REASONING

Unfortunately, "reasoning" is a confusing term, because the root word "reason" is used to mean so many different things. For instance, "reasonable" is often used as a synonym for "sensible," which subtly leads people to feel that reasoning is somehow superior to other modes of thinking.

I look at reasoning as essentially *conscious, logically-based thinking*. I use the term "logically-based" rather than "strictly logical" to indicate my desire for a certain latitude of interpretation. Some types of reasoning try to adhere rigorously to the ground rules of precision, consistency, specificity, and so forth, as exemplified in the formal, deductive (or Aristotelian) brand of reasoning involved in the proof of a geometrical theorem. In the category of reasoning, however, I also want to include instances of less formal adherence to logical ground rules— for example, making plausible inferences and doing heuristic problem-solving. Also included is logically-based thinking about "wholes" or "systems," as well as the more analytic reasoning which emphasizes breaking something down into its component parts for scrutiny.

MUDDLING

Muddling, it seems to me, is *conscious but nonlogical thinking,* which of course makes it somewhat difficult to talk about. It is hard to communicate clearly (logically) about nonlogical matters. Now by nonlogical, I mean something quite different from "illogical" or "unlogical." Nonlogical means that the logical set of ground rules is *not to be applied.* Illogical or unlogical implies that the rules of logic should apply and are being *violated.* Let me use an analogy from the world of sports to clarify the distinction:

The rules for tennis state that a serve is supposed to hit the court first on the *opponent's* side of the net in a *specific* area. If a serve bounces first on the server's side of the net or lands outside the designated area of the opponent's court, the serve is called a "fault"; that is, it violates the rules of tennis.

Suppose we shift to table tennis (a wholly different ball game). Here the rules for a serve state that the ball must hit first on the *server's* side of the court and may than land *anywhere* in the opponent's court. As we watch a table tennis game, we might state that the players were "faulting" on every serve (according to the rules of tennis). Such a comment, however, is not very meaningful, since the game being played is table tennis, not lawn tennis.

While I can't make a complete statement of the ground rules for muddling, it is evident that you won't have much success at the muddling game if you try to play by the logical set of ground rules designed for the reasoning game.

Not all conscious, nonlogical activity, however, merits classification as muddling. Muddling seems to have a purposive element (even though the goal or purpose may be vague), and it appears oriented toward a specific situation or problem (fuzzy as that situation or problem may be). Thus, for instance, daydreaming is certainly a conscious, nonlogical activity; so is listening to music. I would not classify these activities as muddling, however, because they normally don't appear to involve *purposive coping focused on a specific problem,* at the time they occur.

Of course, daydreaming or listening to music can help people solve problems. In fact, any kind of backing off from a problem (e.g., taking a walk or going to sleep) apparently lets the unconscious processes take over for a while. Somehow this intuitive stewing, or incubation, often seems to assist subsequent muddling or reasoning.

A FEW OTHER DESCRIPTIONS OF MUDDLING

Other authors have on occasion described various nonlogical forms of reasoning that resemble to some degree what I am calling muddling. Because these other writers have used somewhat different terms and concepts to describe what they're talking about, their thoughts may shed additional light on what I mean by muddling.

For instance, Edward De Bono in one of his books makes a distinction between "vertical" and "lateral" thinking:

Vertical thinkers take the most reasonable view of a situation and then proceed logically and carefully to work it out. Lateral thinkers tend to explore all the different ways of looking at something, rather than accepting the most promising and proceeding from that. . . .

If you were to take a set of toy blocks and build them upwards, each block resting firmly and squarely on the block below it, you would have an illustration of vertical thinking. With lateral thinking the blocks are scattered around. They may be connected to each other loosely or not at all. But the pattern that may eventually emerge can be as useful as the vertical structure.[1]

[1] Edward De Bono, *New Think* (New York: Basic Books, 1968).

In a later book, De Bono coins a new word ("po") which he suggests be used by someone to signal that he is shifting from the yes-no type of logical thinking into the more exploratory, ambiguous world of lateral thinking where yes-no, right-wrong logic is just not appropriate.

Other writers use terms such as "convergent and divergent" or "approximate and precise" to indicate a similar distinction between two types of thinking. Lateral, divergent, and approximate thinking all involve the willingness to feel one's way and to experiment. All these authors do associate these looser modes of thinking with creativity, but they hasten to add that creativity is more than just thinking in these modes and that not all thinking in these modes is necessarily creative.

A small band of authors working in the field of public administration (such as Charles Lindblom and Aaron Wildavsky) have also devoted much attention to the less rational side of management. Although the writings of these people focus on organizational modes of decision-making in government, many of the concepts seem highly applicable to individual managers in private businesses. The basic position is stated by Lindblom like this:

> To clarify and organize all relevant values, to take an inventory of all important possible policy alternatives, to track down the endless possible consequences of each possible alternative, then to match the multifold consequences of each with the statement of goals—all this runs beyond the capacity of the human mind, beyond the time and energy that a decision maker can afford to devote to problem solving, and in fact beyond the information that he has available. A policy maker, whether an individual or an organization, will become exhausted long before the analysis is exhausted.[2]

Lindblom, and others, go on to talk about the variety of processes that have been developed to cope with this difficult state of affairs. They characterize the overall approach as one of "incrementalism," or working at the margins—that is, a kind of

[2] Charles Lindblom, *The Policy Making Process* (Englewood Cliffs, N.J.: Prentice-Hall, 1968).

pragmatic approach that does not try to deal with whole situations but rather nibbles away at small pieces over time. Some of the key differences they point out between the incremental and more fully analytical, rational approaches are shown below:

INCREMENTAL-PRAGMATIC APPROACH	FULLY ANALYTICAL ECONOMIC APPROACH
Flies under a banner of general ideological rhetoric—e.g., the importance of "service" or "profit."	Specifies clear goals and objectives.
Strategy emerges over time as sum of small decisions.	Starts with overall strategy or grand design.
Bottlenecks are dealt with as they arise.	Problems are planned for in advance.
Means and ends are not kept distinct and become very interwoven.	Ends are isolated first; then appropriate means are sought.
Seeks acceptable, satisfactory, or agreeable moves.	Seeks maximum, optimum moves.
May just move away from something undesirable.	Attempts to move toward what is desired.
Flexibility preferred—i.e., next step open.	Thinks in terms of long-run commitments, and moves may be irreversible.
Improvises, reacts to pressures, is opportunistic.	Attempts comprehensive analysis.

Lindblom concludes that these incremental gambits should not be viewed as narrow-minded and irresponsible; rather, they represent clever and resourceful approaches for "a problem solver who is wrestling bravely with a universe that he is wise enough to know is too big for him."

THE EMOTIONS

Where do emotions and feelings fit into the managerial modes? I suggest that emotions are a kind of direct reaction springing out of our unconscious. We can't control what emotions we're going to feel, but we may be able to control what we do with them once we notice them. At a certain point, then, emotions become an input into thinking and behavior. We can incorporate our emotions in a highly rational, logical manner or in a more nonlogical fashion. From this point of view it is highly questionable to assert that reasoning is a less emotional form of thinking than muddling or intuiting. *The emotions can play an important role in all modes of managerial thinking and behavior.*

Reason as King

POSITIONS AVAILABLE   POSITIONS AVAILABLE
_____

KEY MANAGER WANTED

* Requires strong background in muddling
* Highly developed intuition desirable
* 5–10 years experience in administration
* MBA degree preferred

Send detailed résumé and salary requirements
to Box Z650

You don't find too many recruitment ads like this in *The Wall Street Journal,* or anywhere else for that matter. Ask a manager to describe how he made a decision or why he is taking a certain action. You'll usually get a nicely reasoned answer. Most griping about management is couched in terms of failure to uphold the logical process. Bosses complain about subordinates not reasoning things through before they act; subordinates complain about the boss's failure to set priorities and be consistent.

The great mass of management articles, books, and courses all stress logical problem-solving in one form or another. Much of this educational material emphasizes the use of mathematics, whether it be simple counting and arithmetic or the more esoteric realms of matrix algebra, statistics, and the calculus. The logic and reasoning of mathematics are applied to almost every area of management—purchasing, planning, manufacturing, marketing, and so on. Even in the area of human relations, the manager is urged to logically analyze what he is doing—to motivate personnel by an organized, consistent system of rewards and recognition, or to rationally appraise and assess the strengths and weaknesses of subordinates.

Over and over again the magic formula appears, in basically two versions with only minor modifications or refinements:

1. Define the problem
2. Assess the causes
3. State the standards
4. Develop alternatives
5. Select the best alternative

1. Set objectives and establish priorities
2. Make implementation plans
3. Set milestones with dates
4. Evaluate progress
5. Take corrective actions

These formulas are considered *the* formulas; rarely is it stated that they work only under certain conditions and for certain kinds of situations. The logical ground rules of consistency and precision are, of course, part and parcel of each formula, and constant reminders are issued to be sure objectives are stated precisely, to be sure means are consistent with ends, and so forth.

Formally, reason appears to be king—and appears to be ruling not a tiny fiefdom but all of management country. Now any time a statement like this is made, it is important to consider whether we are talking about how managers actually behave (the descriptive) or how managers ought to behave (the normative). Is the rule of reason descriptive or normative?

In a way, it is both. Certainly the rule of reason is normative, as we saw in our discussions of bossology. Everyone admits that managers sometimes behave illogically or unreasonably, but it is felt that these are temporary deviations, or only minor perturbations; the consensus is that managers should use the reasoning process most of the time. Managers who continually ignore the rule of reason are soon considered incompetent.

THE TENDER TRAP

The stalwart backers of reason as the normative king construct a seemingly impregnable (if somewhat circular) argument. The starting premise is that reason is clearly the best process for any situation. Thus, if reasoning fails to work in an actual situation, the failure can only be attributed to the faulty application of the reasoning process. Possibly the manager didn't fully understand what he was doing, or didn't want to. Perhaps the manager didn't specify things clearly enough, or he was inconsistent, or he overlooked some crucial fact. Maybe he wasn't aware of the latest scientific tool for reasoning out this kind of situation, or was simply unsympathetic to the use of reason and felt safer flying by the seat of his pants. The variety of excuses is endless, but they all imply that if the logical approach had been used and handled properly and pushed far enough, it would not have failed.

Attacking this position is a bit like trying to convince a fatalist that everything is not preordained. When you show the fatalist how you freely chose to do something, he merely replies that your process of choosing, as well as the ultimate choice, were part of a script already written in the sands of time.

The backers of reason are not quite as rigid as the fatalists. They do admit that there are some few situations for which their rational tools have not yet been perfected, but they say it is only a matter of time; in the end, reason will triumph over all. Thus muddling and intuition become processes to be used only by default, and more often than not "de fault" is presumed to be yours, not theirs.

The Power Behind the Throne

In the formal tableau of management, reason may be king. The more informal management scene, however, seems to make muddling a powerful contender for the throne. This informal, off-the-record picture is difficult to paint precisely because it is less formal and clearly articulated; it must be pieced together from wisps of conversation overheard in the washroom, unguarded comments dropped over a few drinks, and brutally frank discussions held behind the closed doors of executive suites.

"Frankly, I'm confused. I really don't know which way to jump."

"All this planning doesn't help that much. Life is just too complicated. There are too many contingencies."

"A lot of times you're better off following your hunches."

"We just don't have time to carefully analyze this thing; we'll simply have to play it by ear."

No doubt you can add to this list of statements with similar examples that you continually hear in your own organization.

Insight into this informal scene can also be gleaned from a series of management "laws" which all proclaim the perversity of nature and the unreasonableness of management. These humorous laws (see box) pop up in a large number of organizations. The content of the laws is often the same, although there is considerable variety in attributed authorship. Experienced managers view these laws not as absurd jokes but rather as caustic truths which exaggerate reality only very slightly, if at all.

THE MANAGEMENT LAWS
OF MURPHY AND HIS FRIENDS

Murphy's Law
If anything can go wrong, it will—
and at the worst possible moment.

Hunt's Law
Everything takes twice as long and costs
50 percent more than the estimates.

Rudin's Law
In a crisis that forces choosing
among alternatives, most people will choose
the worst possible one.

Chisholm's Law
In any collection of data, the figures that are
obviously correct contain the errors.

Finagle's Law
The information we have is not what we want;
the information we want is not what we need;
and the information we need is not available.

The difficulties management scientists encounter in trying to apply their sophisticated logical techniques only provide further evidence for the power of nonlogical thinking. Somehow the management scientists keep finding it hard to isolate a particular problem in an actual situation. Management problems seem to overlap and often lack a clear-cut beginning or end, all of which makes it difficult to apply pure logic or mathematics. Frequently the mathematical models simply cannot handle the wealth of important detail that exists in the real management situation. Many management-science techniques are based on the assumptions that a manager desires to be consistent and that once an inconsistency is pointed out to a manager, he will want to modify his thinking to make it more consistent. Yet there are countless examples of intelligent managers sticking to their inconsistencies quite tenaciously.

The president of a small but rapidly growing mutual fund was discussing a list of potential projects with his management consultant. There were ten projects on the list, and the consultant pointed out that the president's small firm could hardly pursue all these projects at once; some of them would have to be dropped, at least temporarily. The president fully agreed with this.

The consultant then went on to discuss with the president each of the ten projects in turn to decide which projects ought to be held in abeyance. Of course the president had good reasons why each project was absolutely essential. Finally, after an hour or so of analysis, the president said, "Look, the fact of the matter is, we just can't drop any of the projects." The consultant, who was by now feeling very frustrated, replied, "But you agreed that you couldn't handle all of them." "Yes," said the president, "but we just can't drop any of them."

Several decades ago, the computer broke forth on the management scene and was heralded as the living symbol of the ultimate power of reason and management science. It was predicted that a computer would become the chess champion of the world. Today that goal seems nowhere in sight—and chess is a far simpler game than organizational management. The computer was expected to make giant strides in the field of information retrieval, but the categories in which we store information stubbornly seem to defy rigorous systematization. (Just think how often the index of a reference book lacks the very term we want to look up.) Computers were thought to be highly suitable for making translations from one language to another, but success in this area has also been very limited. Even getting a computer to read or respond to just one language (e.g., written or spoken English) has not progressed very far. The semantics and syntax of everyday language seem peculiarly resistant to orderly, consistent, logical programming.

Apparently mathematics, the computer, and management science are simply unable to accomplish many of the things that the human mind can. Some experts on cognitive processes who have tried to pin down the nonlogical abilities of the brain talk about such things as these:

1. Fringe consciousness—a sort of global awareness of alternatives; a zeroing-in process that does not involve actual counting out.
2. Tolerance for ambiguity—reducing various possibilities down as much as the situation requires, without requiring the final result to be absolutely unambiguous.
3. Pattern discovery—which involves distinguishing what is essential from what is unessential by means other than mechanically searching through all possibilities without any previous structuring of the problem.

I would say that what these experts are talking about sounds very much like some aspects of muddling.

Additional evidence for the power of muddling comes from attempts to isolate reliable predictors of managerial success on the job. To date, no research studies have come up with a truly reliable set of predictors. In fact, many management experts have trouble even agreeing on what makes a good manager good. If reasoning ability is so fundamental to good management, the research to date should certainly have uncovered some signs of this. You would expect top management to emphasize reasoning ability in discussing promotions; instead, top management tends to talk about whether the candidate has a good feel for the operations, whether he's good with people, whether he makes a good impression.

It All Depends

Does muddling or reasoning rule the roost? Is muddling more powerful and useful than reasoning, or vice versa? The answer is that it all depends. The meaningful question is, on what does it depend?

THE SITUATION OR PROBLEM

I would like to suggest a series of characteristics that seem to exert considerable influence on whether a given situation calls for muddling or reasoning. Although I will talk about each one separately for the sake of clarity, all the characteristics are certainly interdependent and interrelated. And, while each characteristic does influence which process managers actually use, my comments are more of a normative nature—that is, how each characteristic *should* influence the managerial mode.

1. *People versus things.* Where the human factor looms large, muddling may be more necessary and appropriate. Situations involving inanimate objects (machines, materials, money) seem to be more susceptible to the powers of reasoning. In part this may be because the inanimate aspects of a situation are more easily measured or quantified than the human variables.

2. *Self versus others.* If dealing with people requires more muddling than dealing with inanimate objects, then dealing with oneself seems to require more muddling than dealing with other people. The more personally involved we are in a problem, the more we may need to muddle. I think this occurs partly because other people (like inanimate objects) are outside ourselves, and this makes it easier to draw boundaries. Logical processes do seem most effective in those situations where clear boundaries can be established; this reduces the size of the problem and limits the number of factors to be analyzed.

3. *Size and complexity.* Size means the number of bits and pieces to be dealt with, while complexity means the variety and interrelatedness of those bits and pieces. In the small-to-middle

range of size and complexity, reasoning proves very helpful. However, when a problem is very large and highly complex, the powers of reasoning seem to break down and muddling may be much more appropriate.

4. *Knowledge.* The reasoning process theoretically does not depend on the quantity of information available; it works with whatever you've got. Practically speaking, however, it doesn't make sense to calculate something to the third decimal place when the original data were only valid to the nearest 100. Similarly, when extremely little knowledge or information is available, the application of sophisticated reasoning may simply not be worth the effort. The old computer slogan of GIGO applies: Garbage-in produces garbage-out. Curiously enough, reason may also be replaced by muddling when there is *too much* informa-

tion—that is, when the situation is apparently too large and complex for reasoning to handle.

5. *Certainty.* This is just a special type of knowledge; it means knowing the odds of various possibilities. For instance, not knowing how reliable the rumor of a merger is would be an example of low certainty. Or say we have just hired a new employee who may turn out to be brilliant, mediocre, or incompetent but we really have no idea which outcome is most likely. High uncertainty means a low level of knowledge and a good chance that reasoning will have very limited usefulness.

6. *Control.* Control is essentially the power to change the odds of a particular outcome happening. For instance, we might be able to change the odds of a defective product coming off our production line more easily than we could change the odds of a competitor introducing a new product. In a situation or problem where we control most of the key factors, reasoning may be very helpful in deciding exactly what to do. But when we have very little control over most of the key factors, reasoning is not likely to help as much.

7. *Degree of newness.* Reason seems quite powerless to deal with the very new, essentially because the processes of logic and analysis do little more than spell out the implications of what is already known. Newness means a lack of knowledge; in a new situation, old relationships often don't apply, and we must turn to more nonlogical processes for help.

Ironically, reasoning also runs into problems when a situation involves *very little* newness. Tradition creates ties that bind, but ties that are also very comfortable. Habits are useful precisely because (among other reasons) they're difficult to change. The power of reasoning is not likely to prevail in a situation that shoulders a heavy inheritance from the past.

I believe most managers are somewhat aware of the way in which these seven characteristics of a situation affect (and should affect) the kind of thinking they do. But the managerial modes of thinking and acting depend on another set of factors which managers seem to be much less aware of.

THE MANAGERIAL ROLE OR FUNCTION

I have in mind a particular set of managerial roles or functions that affect (and should affect) the kind of thinking managers do. The roles are:

Exploring		Communicating
and	versus	and
Ideating		Testing

The roles on the left involve trying to learn, search out, or create something new (e.g., an idea for a new product). The roles on the right involve conveying something already discovered or learned, or trying to validate something and convince oneself or others about it (e.g., presenting a new product idea to the boss, or running some market research to check out a product concept).

These two families of functions tend to be mutually exclusive, although a manager certainly can (and often does) jump back and forth very quickly from one to the other. Frequently a manager may think he is communicating or testing and suddenly find himself exploring or ideating, and vice versa.

A more common way of describing managerial roles is in terms of problem-solving, decision-making, and action-taking. Another well-known list of roles is planning, organizing, staffing, directing, and so on. I have no quarrel with these ways of looking at managerial functions, except that they confuse or blur the particular distinction I believe is so crucial. The result is that managers often do not realize that decision-making, planning, or *any function on the standard lists typically involves both exploring or ideating* and *communicating or testing.*

As you may have guessed, I would assert that (1) muddling is most used and most useful for the functions of exploring and ideating; (2) reasoning is most used and most useful for communicating and testing. If most situations that confront managers require both roles, then both muddling and reasoning will be needed.

For instance, the magic formulas shown on page 159 of this

chapter are usually associated exclusively with the techniques of reasoning. But those formulas do not deal with certain crucial matters, particularly those that involve searching out the unknown. How does one go about uncovering or recognizing a problem in the first place? How does one generate all the important alternatives for analysis? How does one anticipate or prevent problems before they arise? These tasks involve exploring or ideating and depend heavily on muddling.

Another important gap in the formulas involves the whole area of values (i.e., standards or criteria against which to evaluate various alternatives). Where do the values come from, and how does one sort out a clash in values?

In the 1960s both Harvard and Yale universities were experiencing enormous pressures for expansion to handle larger numbers of students. Logical analysis brought the two universities to exactly opposite conclusions, because of the differing values from which they started. Stripping down the arguments to their bare essentials, Harvard said we must expand, therefore we will; Yale said we cannot expand, therefore we won't.

As can be seen from this example, reason offers little help in reconciling conflicting values; analysis cannot really tell us what we are interested in or what is most important to us.

Usually the steps in the magic formulas are presented as if they were totally independent. This is simply not the case. For instance, the way we go about searching for problems affects the kind of problems we uncover; the way we define a problem once it is uncovered affects the alternatives we may generate; and the kinds of alternatives we develop often influence our value selection.

There are other interrelationships as well, but the point is that to cope in a completely logical way with a situation, we really need to know everything about the situation before we start, which is obviously an illogical premise. We cannot just analytically follow a problem through step by step and then assemble all the pieces. Somehow we have to alternate between a vision of the whole situation and a look at a particular part of the picture. Logical analysis is simply not sufficient for such a procedure.

Once we know more or less what's going on, reasoning can help us perfect our thinking; it can suggest additional areas for exploration. Once we've developed tentative conclusions, we can check them out by means of logical analysis to see if we uncover anything that makes us change our mind. Reasoning is a good way to keep track of where we've been and what we're doing. Logic can help us organize our thinking so that others will be able to understand our ideas more clearly and not be distracted by all the extraneous material through which we originally plowed.

When logical analysis suddenly helps us resolve a problem, we should not forget all the muddling that preceded the application of reasoning. In fact, when reasoning runs into a dead end, it is usually because of some deficiency in the previous muddling or intuiting activity. Typically a manager must shift back and forth between muddling and reasoning many times in the process of problem-solving. As one idea is clarified or tested by reasoning, this lays the groundwork for the next round of muddling.

Thus the power of muddling versus reasoning all depends—it depends on the character of the situation and on the managerial function being pursued. Unfortunately, the choice between managerial modes is made even more complex because the powers of reasoning are continually evolving.

The Growth of Reason

Management has not been a static profession, and we in the United States are proud to point out the many managerial developments we have pioneered. The primary thrust of almost all this development has been toward extending the power of the reasoning process. But the very existence of so many logical tools makes it difficult for a manager to know when and where reasoning is truly applicable.

New tools for management are introduced every year. Some of them simply make reasoning more efficient: For instance, the computer helps us calculate in a fraction of a minute what formerly required days of reasoning. Increased efficiency, in turn, permits us to extend the power of reason into areas previously deemed too time-consuming or impractical to attack with reason. In addition, certain new techniques of management science have made whole classes of problems accessible to reasoning, where before muddling was the only possibility. For example, take the problem of shipping goods from several factories to several different warehouse locations. Not so many years ago, the only way to handle this problem was for a manager with long years of experience to use his intuition—plus a lot of muddling—to arrive at a fairly good set of decisions. The development of linear programming now provides, in many cases, a thoroughly rational and relatively speedy way to determine the least costly set of decisions for this sort of problem.

Earlier in this century the models of management dealt primarily with the "hard" disciplines of production. As the "soft" sciences of sociology and psychology developed, they were incorporated into the theories of management. Theories of motivation, management by objectives, job enrichment, and other techniques were developed to help managers manage people more rationally and equitably. Some of the techniques were even designed to help the manager understand himself better and thus deal more reasonably with situations in which he was personally involved to a high degree.

All these developments in the power of reasoning have contributed greatly to the manager's formal judgment that reason should be king. At the same time, however, these developments have made it difficult for a manager to know when muddling is really appropriate. Somehow the manager must attempt to keep up with all the latest management-science techniques, or at least know something about the situations in which they might prove useful. But even the experts are considerably divided as to just which techniques are really practical, and as to which techniques have been tested enough to be classified as rational. So a manager's choice among the various thought processes can be very confusing.

As the science of management grows, so an individual

manager develops in his career. Areas where once the manager had to muddle may now be treated much more logically. The continued development of management science, as well as the growth of the individual manager as he proceeds through his career, both conspire to make the boundaries of reasoning and muddling very difficult to perceive.

The Dangerously Unequal Status of Reasoning and Muddling

Both muddling and reasoning are needed and useful—for different situations, for different functions. But reasoning has enormous status and prestige, while muddling often has strongly negative connotations. The "PR boys" have done a whale of a job on the image of reasoning, while muddling has been left skulking in the shadows along with "the heartbreak of psoriasis." Unfortunately, this superior status of reasoning tends to create some unfortunate consequences.

LACK OF AWARENESS

If you want to dumbfound a manager, try asking him under what conditions he feels it appropriate to use reasoning. If you aren't hastily thrown out of his office, the manager will probably first sit in stunned silence and then feebly mumble something like, "I guess I never thought much about it." The formal, high status of reason inhibits our giving much explicit attention to the ways we use reasoning and muddling.

IT'S DIFFICULT FOR OTHERS TO KNOW WHAT WE'RE DOING

The differences between muddling and reasoning hold true not only for the thinking we do by ourselves, but also for the thinking we do with others. Our response to someone we feel is muddling is quite different (or certainly ought to be) from our response to someone we believe to be reasoning. For instance, suppose someone is muddling and throws out a vague idea. If we respond to his half-formed thought with a neatly reasoned criticism, we aren't likely to help along his muddling very much.

Once again the high status and legitimacy accorded to reason make it difficult for others to determine which process we're using. There's a natural tendency for others to assume that we're

reasoning most of the time, particularly because custom pre-
scribes that in public we reason; muddling is something we're
apparently supposed to do in private, if at all. Even when we're
inconsistent and ramble, other people will tend to interpret this
as evidence of poor reasoning rather than as an indication that
we're muddling. It's especially hard for a *boss* to convince others
that he's muddling. Any casual idea coming from the boss is
often acted on as if it were a firm, final recommendation—"no
sooner heard than done."

Occasionally we may drop very explicit clues that we desire
to muddle. We use such phrases as these:

"Let's just kick this thing around."

"Now, of course, I'm talking off the top of my head."

"Let me bounce this off you."

But even in the presence of these clues, other people feel bound
by the ground rules of logic and will usually silently refuse our
invitation to muddle. They continue to assume that *they* will be
judged on logical grounds, even though we are muddling. Of
course, the refusal of others to believe we are muddling is sometimes justified, because the phrases cited above are often used as
a security device—we aren't really muddling at all, but just want
a way to save face if the other person should find our idea unreasonable.

In fact, we drop false clues in the other direction as well.
Sometimes when we're muddling we cloak it in the garb of reason
because we feel guilty or inadequate about having to muddle;
that is, we fall prey to the prestige and acceptability of reason.

Quite often the problem is not so much a matter of false
clues as it is of ambiguous clues. Even when we're aware of
which process we're using and want to convey that fact, what we
say may not clearly indicate which mode we're in. For instance,
suppose I say to a subordinate, "What do you think of hiring
fewer people and going to more overtime?" Now it may be that
the overtime idea is just one of many floating around in my head
—I'm exploring a problem and want to develop other ideas; I
want to muddle. On the other hand, I may have carefully thought
about the problem and now want to test out my conclusions. In

fact, I may not even be testing; I may have reached my decision and am merely communicating it diplomatically to my subordinate.

Actions can be equally hard to interpret. Suppose I cut the travel budget of a salesman. I may have carefully analyzed the salesman's travel schedules and concluded they are poorly organized and wasteful. In other words, I've cut his travel budget as a logical way to force him to plan his travel more efficiently. On the other hand, I might be muddling: That is, I need to increase profitability and am experimenting with any number of moves to see what kinds of results they produce.

It can be even more confusing if we rapidly shuttle back and forth between reasoning and muddling (though on many occasions such oscillation is perfectly appropriate). Actually, the most telling problem is that most of the time we're not really aware ourselves of which process we're using, so it's hardly fair to expect others to know what we're doing. In light of all this, it's no wonder that others find it easier and safer to simply assume that we're reasoning all the time.

MISUSE

If we're not always aware of which thinking process we're using, we also don't devote much attention to considering which thinking process would be most appropriate. Without our fully realizing it, the highly positive image of reasoning draws us into trying to reason in activities where muddling might be more effective.

The directors of a small electronics firm had for some time been trying to sell the president on the need for making some long-range plans. (Long-range in this case was one year ahead.) The president insisted he didn't need to be sold. He really wanted to plan; he had read several books on the subject and had even attended a short seminar on planning. Yet somehow the president never got around to producing any plans.

One evening over cocktails with an astute business friend, the president discussed his difficulties with planning. The friend suggested that the president had some basic misconceptions about what was involved in planning. *Plans* might be detailed, specific, and logical, but much of *planning* wasn't. The friend argued that planning actually involved a lot of groping around, that objectives were not a starting point but the result of playing around with many possibilities. The friend also pointed out that the president seemed to be approaching planning as an all-or-nothing affair, which it didn't need to be. In fact, nobody ever planned everything all at once.

The president was amazed. He had never thought about planning in this way. He had been attempting to plan in a purely logical and analytical fashion, had been getting nowhere, and as a result had been avoiding the whole matter. After a few months of muddling for an hour here and an hour there, the president finally produced his first set of plans—primitive and incomplete to be sure, but something he could use as a take-off point for further thinking. At last the president was planning.

FOOLING OURSELVES

Sometimes we choose to muddle because this process allows us to overlook major conflicts or sidestep a lot of troublesome details. We find it easier to live with these unresolved issues when we leave them fuzzy or ill-defined, although this, of course, doesn't make them any less serious. Thus we sometimes fool ourselves by muddling.

We often fool ourselves just as badly when we reason, though in a different way. I have suggested that a purely logical approach is not feasible in most real situations. In order to reason we must make a number of simplifying assumptions, and we must leave out a certain number of factors to reduce the complexity of the problem to reasonable proportions. In short, we shape the problem to fit the capabilities of reasoning. But after a long and tortuous analysis, we tend to forget all the arbitrary shaping we did along the way. For instance, we may have realized that certain qualitative factors needed to be considered but temporarily put them aside in order to deal with the more quantifiable elements of the situation. Often, however, we never get back to those qualitative factors.

The power of reasoning is very seductive. We come to fully believe in the conclusions of our reasoning, despite all the qualifications we make during the process. As the noted essayist and naturalist Joseph Wood Krutch once remarked, "Logic [may be] only the act of going wrong with confidence."

On Behalf of Muddling

In the preceding section we saw in a number of ways just how dangerous the unequal statuses of reasoning and muddling can be. At the very least, shouldn't we take some conscious steps to redress the balance and bolster the formal status of muddling? For instance, why not start by assuming that most management situations are fuzzy; if we don't see the fuzz, then we've probably overlooked or forgotten something important. Even if we're skittish about publicly admitting the fuzz, we can at least take cognizance of it privately. (The chapter on discretion developed some of the implications of doing this in delegation and management by objectives.)

Why not begin to assume that most of the time we, and others, are muddling rather than reasoning. Let's switch the burden of proof around; *Muddling is to be assumed until proven to the contrary.* (The chapter on reorganization proposed a similar switch by viewing reorganization as a form of exploration that involves a good deal of muddling.) We'll deal quite differently (and probably more effectively) with our bosses or anyone else if we realize that they're muddling most of the time. (Many of the suggestions in the chapter on subordination sprang from this approach.)

We could even start to talk in public a little more about muddling. This doesn't mean continuously pointing out to our bosses and colleagues that they're terribly muddled. We can pick and choose our spots to let the topic of muddling creep into the conversation. It's not nearly as risky as we imagine. In fact, explicitly acknowledging the need to muddle often generates a highly audible sigh of relief.

Perhaps it's time that management training take more cognizance of muddling instead of exclusively promoting worship of the demi-god of reason. Perhaps professional trainers could be instrumental in developing improved methods for muddling.

(These notions are part of what the chapter on training was about.)

UNNATURAL MUDDLING

We start out life muddling, not reasoning. It takes many years of schooling to develop our reasoning ability, and even after that we continue to muddle for much of our lives. Why is it we have such a problem with regard to muddling, if it's just doing what comes naturally?

The point is that while certain types of muddling may come naturally, effective management requires a special brand of muddling. Our natural muddling takes its own sweet time, while management muddling involves rigorous time constraints and deadlines. Natural muddling runs into trouble when it must be condensed, when a manager simply cannot wait for the natural sorting-out process to occur. Some techniques for more organized muddling (or management muddling) were the subject of the first chapter of this book.

Over the longer run we can hope that research will further clarify the ground rules for muddling and begin to distinguish between different varieties of organized muddling. For instance, dealing with experts (Chapter 5) may require one kind of muddling, while fiddling with figures may require another.

We can hope to develop new ways of increasing a manager's ability to muddle. We might discover that certain kinds of organization structures help or hinder effective muddling. We might even find ways of moving certain things now handled by intuition into the domain of muddling (just as we've learned how to move certain things from muddling into the realm of reasoning).

We might develop clearer boundaries for both reasoning and muddling—boundaries that would help us know better when and where each mode is most appropriate. Finally, we might learn more about how to combine the various processes, since the great majority of management problems will continue to require a combination of intuiting, muddling, and reasoning.

Above all, by formally recognizing the existence of fuzziness, we will realize why management isn't the way it's supposed to be—why it probably *shouldn't* be the way it's supposed to be. We'll learn that the problems caused by fuzziness are not to be avoided at all costs, but instead are problems to be worked on and lived with. Perhaps most important of all, we will come to find that the fuzzy side of management not only poses serious problems but opens up unusual *opportunities* as well—and only then may we claim to fully understand what properly unbusinesslike management is all about.